Illustration

A Theoretical & Contextual Perspective

Illustration

A Theoretical & Contextual Perspective

Alan Male

ava |Academia
the environment of learning

An AVA Book
Published by AVA Publishing SA
Rue des Fontenailles 16
Case Postale
1000 Lausanne 6
Switzerland
Tel: +41 786 005 109
Email: enquiries@avabooks.ch

Distributed by Thames & Hudson (ex-North America)
181a High Holborn
London WC1V 7QX
United Kingdom
Tel: +44 20 7845 5000
Fax: +44 20 7845 5055
Email: sales@thameshudson.co.uk
www.thamesandhudson.com

Distributed in the USA & Canada by:
Watson-Guptill Publications
770 Broadway
New York, New York 10003
USA
Fax: 1-646-654-5487
Email: info@watsonguptill.com
www.watsonguptill.com

English Language Support Office
AVA Publishing (UK) Ltd.
Tel: +44 1903 204 455
Email: enquiries@avabooks.co.uk

ISBN 2-940373-51-5 and 978-2-940373-51-2

10 9 8 7 6 5 4 3 2 1

Design by Peter Bennett
Image Research by Clare Elsom

Production by AVA Book Production Pte. Ltd., Singapore
Tel: +65 6334 8173
Fax: +65 6259 9830
Email: production@avabooks.com.sg

Illustration: *a definition*
Applied Imagery; a 'working art'
that visually communicates context
to audience.

Preface

This book examines the measure of contextual operation regarding contemporary illustration practice. It also seeks to provide an exemplification of theoretical and intellectual processes necessary for the production of accomplished work. It does *not* emphasise matters of commercial or business practice, nor aspects of media or practical concern such as rendering techniques or technical processes. These issues are best served by volumes specific and dedicated to these subjects. Aimed predominantly at final year undergraduate and post-graduate students there is assignation to a defined understanding and application regarding all modes of project development, including research, subject matter, conceptual processing, context and audience, analysis and visual language.

The discipline of illustration was once an exclusive club with practitioners remaining firmly within the confines of 'commercial art'. However, the emergence of stock art and the impact and advancement of digital technology have instigated a 'changing face' regarding the discipline of illustration, and many illustrators have had to re-evaluate their practice. Today, there is much emphasis on the acquisition of transferable skills and the ability to multitask. It is not uncommon for individuals to proclaim a status comprising 'illustrator-writer', 'illustrator-designer' and with some more unusual, varied and disparate combinations.

Illustration practice is not judged purely by visual literacy and technical qualities, but is a discipline that is firmly established as one that engenders the best intellectual engagement with subject matter, problem solving and visual communication. Illustration can also be applied to anything and is not driven purely by fad or trend. The global community is its potential audience.

This book explores the breadth of use for illustration and does not discriminate. It presents a collective of five distinct and separate contextual domains that constitutes the role of illustration: documentation, reference and instruction; commentary; storytelling; persuasion; and identity.

Whilst engaged in what is broadly an objective and pragmatic approach to processes and outcomes, illustrators can and do proact authorship and expertise regarding many aspects of contextual operation. It is this concern that provides a certain platform and underpinning to much regarding an examination of contemporary practice. The notion of illustrator as 'colouring-in technician' must be discarded!

6 How to get the most out of this book

This book is divided into four chapters.
The first chapter examines 'Education', the
second 'The Nature of Imagery', and the
third 'The Role of Illustration'. The final
chapter is a thorough 'Appendix' containing
a 'Project Brief Development Checklist', a
'Research and Reference Gathering
Checklist', a 'Project Assessment and Review
Checklist', a 'Project Appraisal, Critique and
Reflection', and a 'Project Proposal
Proforma', together with information on
where to get representation and how to put
together a portfolio. Also included here is a
detailed glossary and bibliography.

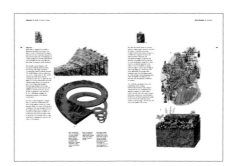

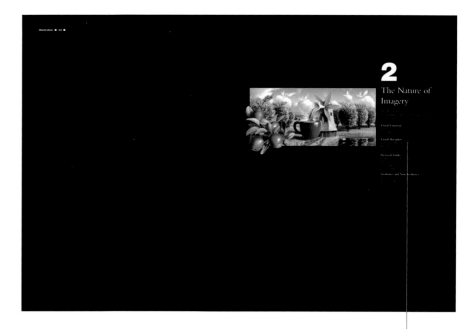

Chapter openers look
like this and contain a
mini table of contents
for quick reference.

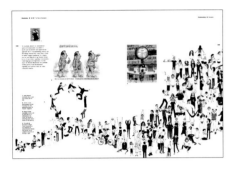

Each chapter is broken down by relevant subheadings that are accompanied by insightful text.

Captions are numbered to accompany relevant images. Each caption includes the name of the illustrator, together with additional information about the image.

Pull quotes are used to visually add pace, and to highlight certain things the author is saying.

An enormous selection of very diverse styles of illustration is featured to visually accompany the text. Each image has a number reference that corresponds to a relevant caption.

Running heads appear along the top of each page to aid navigation throughout the book.

8   **CONTENTS**

10

Introduction

1

In one form or another, illustration has been in existence for centuries, but has only been recognised as a distinct discipline fairly recently. In the USA its importance and recognition was granted by the founding of the Society of Illustrators in 1901, but it is still scorned by sections of the fine art community because of its commercial grounding. As a visual language and medium it has, over the years, had many loose and disparate descriptions from painting, engraving, commercial art, cartoons, pictures in books and drawing. It is often confused with other disciplines, most notably that of graphic design and fine art, perhaps because there is an occasional overlap. However, there is a distinct core that is unlike anything else and it is this that defines its 'raison d'être'. Illustration is about communicating a specific contextualised message to an audience. It is rooted in an objective need, which has either been generated by the illustrator or a commercial based client to fulfil a particular task. It is the measure and variety of these different tasks that makes the discipline of illustration such an influential visual language.

Previous generations were informed, educated or had their opinions swayed by commissioned paintings – pictures of glorious victories in battle; scenes of outrageous sporting endeavour; religious icons and heavenly splendour; flattering or deliberately not-so-flattering portraits. Contemporary generations are also greatly influenced by illustration and because of the medium of print, moving images and more recently the digital revolution, accessibility is everywhere. This also defines a distinctive feature of the discipline in that nearly every image classed as illustration is reproduced and distributed often on an international scale. So, what

messages are impressed on society by illustration? Most people have been influenced by children's books. These have been described as 'holding the key to worlds locked inside the imagination, as well as depicting worlds that exist but cannot be seen.' Children's picture books, whether fiction or non-fiction feed us attitudes and information and help to develop our visual senses and intellect. The creative possibilities of illustration are limitless. Away from a contextual need for literal truth it becomes unfettered by reality and one's imagination is free to create images and conjure up atmospheres. An illustration can also shock a newspaper reader into taking notice of a contentious argument, it can give a bland, faceless company a new identity and it can send any product into a fantasy world that might appeal to a potential buyer.

2

1. George Cruikshank had a long and industrious career during the 19th century and is particularly renowned for illustrating early works by Charles Dickens. This is 'The Burglary' from Oliver Twist. George Cruikshank (British, 1792–1878), The Burglary, 1838, 10.2 x 9.8 (image), 23.9 x 13.8 cm (sheet), Fine Arts Museums of San Francisco, Achenbach Foundation for Graphic Arts, 1963.30.32698.

2. N.C.Wyeth was one of the earliest and most successful American illustrators of the early 20th century and whose original artworks can be found at the Society of Illustrators in New York. This is a book cover from 1916.

3. Saul Bass was an exponent of what many called 'commercial art', a blend of graphic design and illustration. This is a film poster from 1961. 'One, Two, Three' © 1961 Metro-Goldwyn-Mayer Studios Inc. All Rights Reserved. Courtesy of MGM CLIP+STILL.

4. Joel Stewart's children's book illustrations of 'Pobble' provide fantastical interpretations.

3

11

The Illustrator What are the qualities, attributes and skills that make for a successful, practising illustrator? This question is particularly relevant today where there is shifting and blurring of boundaries between disciplines, particularly in the creative and media industries. To begin with, it is widely acknowledged that one of the initial aspects of an illustrator's education is to do with the acquisition of practical skills. The operative skills that are associated with contemporary illustration practice, involves the utilisation of a range of media, both traditional and increasingly digital as, for example, promoting oneself by way of a website has become the norm. Sound academic drawing practise is also an essential underpinning for most aspects of illustration, irrespective of the visual language or style one is associated with. The externalisation and visualisation of concepts and ideas are best deployed by the process of drawing. The application of creative processing to problems of visual communication and the innovative use of design and conceptualisation are also essential, facilitated by the natural 'gift' of visual intelligence. It is however, unfortunate that some commissioning art directors and illustration tutors place importance on the superficiality of visual language and the commercial constraints placed upon it to conform to trends and fashion. In education, the student illustrator is often under pressure to 'break new ground' and push the boundaries of the subject. This usually means the production of so-called 'innovative' mark-making that in reality does nothing to consider the real business of illustration.

In a professional context, successful, forward-thinking illustrators no longer operate the way many did and some still do, as merely 'colouring in technicians', receiving briefs that are heavily directed and prescribed regarding content and overall visual concept. Many illustrators 'take the lead', or are given it, in terms of directing a project or commission. This has a significant bearing on the professional process and means that the best illustrators are often educated, socially and culturally aware. They need to have knowledge of, be authoritative about and have empathy for a great many topics and subjects, particularly those the illustrator may be required to engage with as part of a brief. They also need to be mindful of current affairs and opinion, be contemporary with society at large and current trends in visual

language and media. Illustrators need to have knowledge, understanding and insight regarding the context within which they are working, the subject matter they are engaged with, and be able professionals working within the parameters and needs of the market place and target audiences. They need to utilise a breadth of intellectual and practical skills that might once be regarded as transferable from other disciplines but considered essential if the illustrator has ambitions to transcend the role of commissioned 'hack'.

4

1

Education

Successful, forward-thinking illustrators need to be educated, socially and culturally aware communicators utilising a breadth of intellectual and practical skills.

1

14   Education

The acquisition of practical skills such as traditional, autographic rendering techniques and digital, new technology-based skills, is essential regarding the education of the illustrator, but must also be regarded as a form of training associated with the vocational aspects of illustration and encountered early in one's development. As the illustrator enters the final leg of their education, the development of a personal iconography through drawing, media exploration and visual interpretation should be more or less established. It has to be considered an almost superficial activity compared to the depth of engagement required when dealing with the complex issues of creative processing and research when solving problems of contextualised visual communication.

The Programme of Work

For advanced level study in higher education, the projects and assignments should not replicate the heavily art directed and prescribed briefs given to professional illustrators by certain clients nor merely be in place to provide further development of visual language or technical skills. Work undertaken should provide a platform to demonstrate a systematic understanding of knowledge and a critical awareness of new insights, much of which is at, or informed by, the forefront of the discipline of illustration. This work should enable the student illustrator to demonstrate a practical understanding and application of established methodologies regarding research and enquiry, and use it to create and interpret knowledge. The projects should also enable the student to demonstrate self-direction and originality in tackling and solving problems, and act autonomously in planning and implementing tasks. These challenges are commensurate with the notion that successful, forward-thinking illustrators need to be educated, socially and culturally aware communicators utilising a breadth of intellectual and practical skills.

'Successful, forward-thinking illustrators need to be educated, socially and culturally aware communicators utilising a breadth of intellectual and practical skills.'

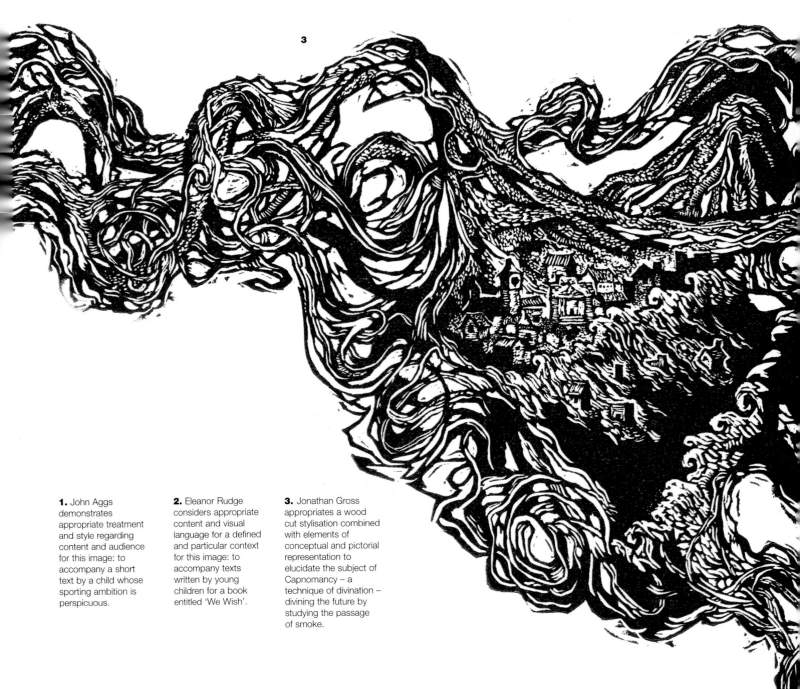

2

The programme of work undertaken should be negotiated and based on personal choice, such as a particular interest in a topic and/or having empathy and aptitude for a certain context. The principal aim of the assignment should always be to solve a problem of visual communication. The task set should be clear and unambiguous and its rationale should be to advance knowledge and understanding, and develop intellectual and practical skills to a high level.

3

1. John Aggs demonstrates appropriate treatment and style regarding content and audience for this image: to accompany a short text by a child whose sporting ambition is perspicuous.

2. Eleanor Rudge considers appropriate content and visual language for a defined and particular context for this image: to accompany texts written by young children for a book entitled 'We Wish'.

3. Jonathan Gross appropriates a wood cut stylisation combined with elements of conceptual and pictorial representation to elucidate the subject of Capnomancy – a technique of divination – divining the future by studying the passage of smoke.

1

16   Developing the Brief

An illustration assignment or project brief at this advanced level of study should contain three distinct and clearly defined directives.

The Rationale – why you are undertaking this task;
The Aim – what it is you are going to do? And;
The Objectives – how you intend to proceed; a clear list of methodologies to be employed.

The Rationale

There should be a theme or body of knowledge and an identifiable need for visual communication. What has informed this choice and why?

The project should be an example of one of the following:

a. A professional practice area of context. Examples may be: information given by way of a publishing medium; promotional and persuasive material to be displayed publicly in a large printed format; narrative fiction for a young audience; corporate material produced as moving imagery and embodied into an internet website. The context must be clearly established – the job of work the illustration(s) is/are intended to do – as this determines a substantial part of the problem-solving process.

b. A question that needs answering, creating a need to research and present new knowledge. If so, is the audience specialist or non-specialist? This would be a scholarly research-based thesis that manifests as a visual essay and contains substantial critical analysis, a review of the subject's historical and contemporary placement, and a conclusion expounded by both written and visual work.

1,2a,b,c,d. Juan Moore has considered a defined theme and context with a series of originally conceived, designed and illustrated posters.

3,4. Jason Cripps has developed projects based on an enquiring, esoteric, yet humorous approach, but nonetheless grounded in contextual need. This is an image for a book of quotes.

'The project should be an example of one of the following:

either a professional practice area of context or a question that needs answering, creating a need to research and present new knowledge.'

2a 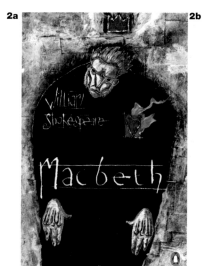   **2b**

3

The rationale should convey how much knowledge or empathy the student already has regarding the theme of the project. It may be something that one has engaged with in a previous project and the intention is to develop this further and produce a more challenging 'follow-on'. There may be some extra-curricular association or experience that can provide additional insights. Choices made at this stage may inform and assist future development regarding one's post-higher education ambitions and although academically and professionally challenging, should broadly reflect interests, capabilities and aptitudes.

The Aim
The nature and full extent of the project should be clearly set out stating what the outcome is to be and what will manifest at its conclusion, for example, the amount of development work, presentation visuals/dummies, artworks/finished imagery.

The Objectives
As well as stating how one intends to action the proposed work, there should also be a clear timetable laid out. The objectives should identify new knowledge outcomes and how the intended work will facilitate professional and academic development.

4

2c

2d

1

18   Answering the Brief

The initial process to undergo is one of analysis. What is the problem of visual communication that needs to be solved and what is it that one is actually communicating, to whom and for whom? First, identify and understand the context. What is the nature of the task required of the imagery? Also, what is the content and subject matter that is being dealt with? Is there a need for research and/or to find out more than is already known about the subject? 'Only an intelligent analysis of the information generated by the briefing process can lead to an appropriate visual solution.' Richard Steel, 'Illuminations: Solving Design Problems Through Illustration'.

Contexts

The foremost assertion is a philosophical one relating to a definition of what the discipline of illustration actually is. The author has already described it thus in previous publications as a 'working art' that visually communicates context to audience (traditionally through drawing). It demands an approach that is both objective and pragmatic regarding its working processes and outcomes. Unlike fine art, the discipline it is most frequently confused with or compared to, illustration is not necessarily cultivated for its own sake and is not meant as a pandering to any intrinsic pleasures it affords the minds and emotions that might experience it. So, without a context, an image cannot be described as being an illustration. The contexts of working practice, in other words, the different 'jobs of

1a

2

3

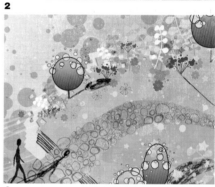
4

5

The contextual domains of illustration practice are represented by the six images depicted here.

1,1a. Information: David Bain's farm map provides colourful yet easily accessible information regarding directions and whereabouts.

2. Commentary: Christopher Burge's editorial illustration makes provocative comment regarding vegetarianism; 'If God intended us to be vegetarians why did he make animals out of meat?'

3. Narrative Fiction: Levi Pinfold has illustrated his own story entitled 'The Magic Book'. Evocative and pictorially representational.

4. Identity: Yee Ting Kuit has produced a corporate image for a chain of garden centres.

5. Persuasion: Greg Reed's three-dimensionally constructed image promotes a New Zealand local authority stance on pollution; 'Poison the sea. Poison me'.

6,7. Maria Raymondsdotter has provided this image for a specific target audience regarding age group and locality; a promotional illustration for a regional rail company.

6

work' illustration does is paramount to understanding its relevance and importance as a modern medium of visual communication. Illustration is seen everywhere, its potential and working possibilities are endless. It influences the way we are informed and educated, what we buy and how we are persuaded to do things. It gives us opinion and comment. It provides us with entertainment and tells us stories. The best illustrations accomplish the successful and where appropriate, creative transfer of particular messages to prescribed audiences. There are five generally and broadly recognised contextual domains: **Information**, **Commentary**, **Narrative Fiction**, **Persuasion** and **Identity**. It is likely that any brief initiated here will conform to at least one of these domains, although it is possible for any mix of combinations.

Audiences

Having an understanding of the audience is essential for the successful transfer of messages. Fundamental to this is to know exactly what type of response is required of the audience and whether or not they would 'buy' the message being communicated. Is the requirement for a straightforward message that is objective in nature such as factual, informative material, or is there a need to be subjective and provoke an emotive response whereby the audience sees something in the content and message of the illustration they normally would not see elsewhere? Visual communication relies on semiotics. This is where the audience interprets and translates signs and symbols, often by association and the deciphering of these meanings can be subconscious.

We live in a multicultural age and the creative industries in which the discipline of illustration is firmly embedded plays across all continents of the earth. This has a significant bearing on who an illustrator's audience is for any given brief. Many children's books for example, both fiction and non-fiction, will only be produced by a United Kingdom publisher if they have secured deals with companies in North America and other countries. This can impact greatly on the content of imagery and messages that are imparted. Therefore

7

'Illustration influences the way we are informed and educated, what we buy and how we are persuaded to do things. It gives us opinion and comment. It provides us with entertainment and tells us stories.'

1

20 the illustrator has to adopt a multinational and cross-cultural approach. What might be acceptable material to convey to Northern Europeans or Americans may not be either understood or appreciated by nationalities elsewhere. With reference to non-fiction books, especially for children, the content of these publications has become more authoritative with much emphasis on accuracy of information and an affirmation of ethics and precepts related to subject matter such as respect and support for ecology, conservation and the environment, an avoidance of jingoism and prejudice regarding social and historical material, and an application of equality and fairness regarding culture, race and gender. Many publishers take the editorial line that it is essential as an illustrator that one respects and adheres to these maxims.

The advertising industry tends to be prescribed and sometimes produces campaigns that are regionalised within a single country. The message is often to persuade a particular type of customer to purchase a product best suited to them only. In this context, it can be expedient to categorise the audience by gender, age, social background and income.

Clients
As previously described, one of the defining features of the discipline of illustration is that its need has either been generated by the illustrator or by a commercial-based client. If it is self-generated, there will be a requirement for commercial outlets, such as publishers willing to provide production, distribution and therefore accessibility to the potential customer/audience. However, with a certain amount of business acumen it can be possible to self-publish and establish one's own appropriate marketing opportunities. In this circumstance, self-publishing does not mean 'self-indulgence' or the production of overtly 'personal work'. It is worth observing

2

'The concept of the illustrator as a specialist or authority on a particular subject or as an originator of either fiction and/or non–fiction material has become widely accepted.'

3

4

1,2. Publishing;
Children's Non-fiction:
The author designed and illustrated this complete book including the cover; 'Spiders and their Web Sites'.

3. Publishing;
Children's Fiction:
'Hungry! Hungry! Hungry!' illustrated by Paul Hess.

4. Publishing;
Quality Non-fiction:
Chris Griffen's cover for Robert Opie's 'The 1950s Scrapbook'.

5

that whatever genre of written or visual work being published, a prerequisite to determine its credibility would be that it is either peer reviewed and/or subjected to editorial quality control. Being distanced from the objectivity of a defined context negates the rationale of the brief. However, as has been stated before regarding the formulation of negotiated projects in an educational circumstance, initiating a brief of this sort does not mean the exclusion of personal interests. The concept of the illustrator as a specialist or authority on a particular subject or as an originator of either fiction and/or non-fiction material has become widely accepted. With regards to clients operating commercially, there is no need here to dwell upon the subtlety of difference between individuals working within a range of different organisations. Neither is there a need to analyse their role and function or to examine how they actually commission illustration. It is, however, essential to know and understand the outlets for illustration. In a broad sense these 'outlets' can be described as clients. The following list represents an overview of principal outlets for the commissioning of illustration:

Publishing: Books

Children's Books
Non-fiction: Popular and/or specialist reference; trade and/or national curriculum. Fiction: Picture books for very young to teenage children.

Quality Non-Fiction
Encyclopaedias or single subject 'Coffee Table': Popular subjects such as cookery, gardening, sport, natural history, motoring, biographies, etc.

General Fiction
Hardback and paperback, mainly for adults.

Specialist
Technical reference, obscure subjects.

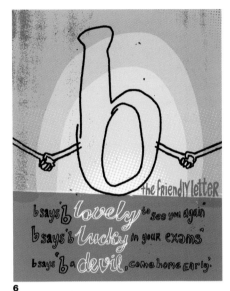

6

7

8

9

5,9. Publishing;
Specialist:
Neil Packer provided this image for the cover of a specialist book about cookery; 'Regional Foods of Southern Italy'.

6. Advertising;
'Above the Line':
Andy Smith's illustration promoting a mobile phone company; 'B is a Friendly Letter'.

7. Publishing;
General Fiction:
Andy Bridge illustrated this cover wrap for 'Gringo Soup'.

8. Publishing;
Magazines & Newspapers:
Frazer Hudson's editorial illustration providing comment about divorce; '50/50 Split'.

22

Publishing: Magazines and Newspapers
Editorials
General, specific or 'life style'; articles and commentaries.

Advertising
'Above the line'; in print and/or moving image.

Design Groups
'Below the line'; point of sale, company reports, packaging, corporate material, internet website design, etc.

Multimedia
Moving image; animation, post-production, film, digital imaging.

Miscellaneous
Institutions, organisations or private individuals not associated with above; public services, local or national government, academic institutions.

1,3. Lewis Campbell uses spontaneous and vigorous drawing as the basis for his award-winning animation stills from 'Capoeira'.

2. Ricca Kawai has produced images for the packaging of a series of medicinal products.

4. Jill Calder's image 'Freeing Capital, Controlling Costs'.

'Having an understanding of the audience is essential for the successful transfer of messages.'

4

1

24   **Subject Matter**

The visual language that is illustration can be used to depict or represent anything. It is therefore essential that the illustrator is equipped to engage with the subject matter and content of imagery being conceived and produced. But what is this engagement and how can it be successful?

Illustrators inform, narrate and comment in the same way writers might. The craft of using the written word can be applied to anything and covers the same contexts of practice as illustration. Writers tend to have specialist knowledge or particular creative skills appropriate for their context of operation. They acquire expertise and knowledge of their subject, whatever that might be applied to, from scriptwriting, journalism, narrative fiction or technical authorship. Successful illustrators must do likewise and become authoritative and qualified regarding the components of their work. The pursuit of knowledge and information is a prerequisite to eminent, professional illustration practice.

Writing and illustration are more than just contiguous, they are one and the same. The link is intrinsic as can be exemplified by the fact that 50 per cent of picture books and early readers' fictional narrative is now written and illustrated by the same person. This does however highlight an inaccurate representation of illustration shown by inclusion as one of the disciplines within the roster belonging to the Chartered Society of Designers, a UK-based professional body. Here, illustration is out of place by association with design-based disciplines such as interior and functional 3D design. These do not practice any form of contextualised visual communication. It should be more appropriate for illustrators to

2

'The pursuit of knowledge and information is a prerequisite to eminent, professional illustration practice.'

1,2. Eivind Bøvor's interest and knowledge regarding certain aspects of history and archaeology has led to the research and visual reconstruction of a specific Iron Age hill fort near Truro, Cornwall, UK.

3,4. Juliet Percival has utilised knowledge gained from her science-based undergraduate degree to forge a career in medical illustration.

3

be professionally associated with sources of information regarding their own practice. The Society of Children's Book Writers and Illustrators is one such organisation and the Guild of Natural Science Illustrators is another. Sharing knowledge and experience is invaluable and association with one's peers can provide a rich source of potential references for subjects to be illustrated.

At undergraduate and to a certain extent postgraduate level, it is important to keep certain options open and not narrowly specialise too much in any particular subject or visual language, especially early in one's development. It is difficult to predict what doors of opportunity may open either before graduation or after.

The aim for 'individualism' can be a more appropriate course of action which can support innumerable options and ways of augmenting one's abilities and aptitudes.

It has been known to happen for someone to seek the undergraduate study of illustration having already acquired an equivalent qualification in a specialist subject academically some distance from art and design practice and possibly embedded within the broad domains of science and culture. Specific examples might be Human Anatomy, Prehistoric Archaeology or Applied Mathematics. Often, these individuals wish to utilise and disclose their expert knowledge by way of illustration.

But how else does one acquire knowledge of subject matter? The key to this question is fairly simple: engage in research, have an enquiring mind and possess a general desire for learning.

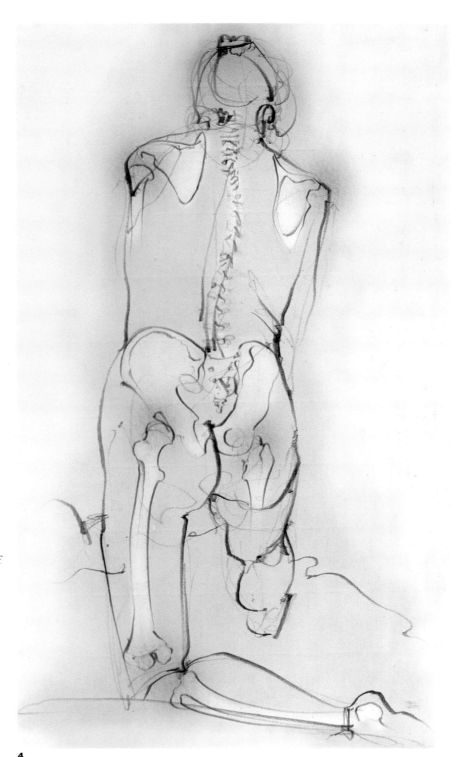

4

1

26   The Conceptual Process

The possession of a comprehensive and cognitive understanding of the brief with fully researched and assembled aspects of subject matter defines the moment to begin solving the problem of visual communication. The problem could be to design and illustrate anything from a multitude of image requirements and media.

The following are two examples of quite extreme outcomes that have a bearing on the intensity and volume of the work required:

A single image to be reproduced in an established or pre-designed publication with layout and placement of illustration predetermined, for example an editorial illustration in a magazine.

A complete 32-page book with full-colour illustrations throughout, including cover with a requirement for interactive devices such as 'pop-ups'.

Brainstorming and Creative Processing

Whatever the complexity of the brief, the initial process of initiating and generating ideas and concepts is basically the same and the most common practice is to brainstorm and record all thoughts and notions by way of written and/or visual note-taking. This way of working is an undertaking that cannot easily be taught. Authors often complain of 'writer's block' and comparative situations can easily arise for illustrators. By taking inspiration and developing this into a creative visual idea is not something that can be done by rote. It cannot be compared with performing a simple, repetitive operation. However, it does have to be done and one's professional circumstance demands it. The blank page in a sketch- or notebook can provoke psychological anxieties. This can, in part be alleviated by the instantaneous recording of the first thought that transpires no matter how trivial or seemingly unconnected with the brief. From plain origins, experimentation can evolve and from this appropriate associations can manifest.

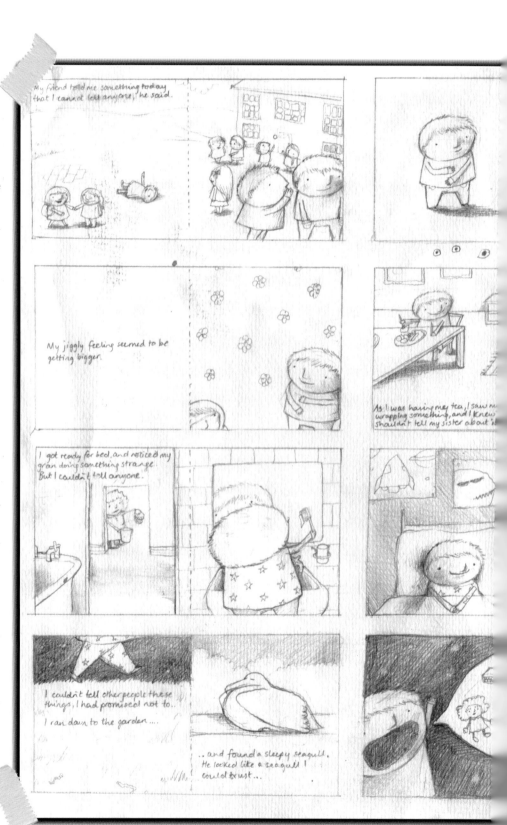

2

'Taking inspiration and developing this into a creative visual idea is not something that can be done by rote.'

1. Developmental drawings by Nigel Owen for an editorial illustration about wine to be published in the 'Independent' newspaper.

2. Hannah Cumming has conceived from scratch an original fictional narrative for a young audience and created this initial storyboard for considerations to be made regarding content and narrative pace and flow.

1

28 Explore both literal and lateral thoughts and ideas and create spider diagrams, lists and simple or complex sketches. The creative process should start to flow more readily at this point and more concrete and defined ideas could materialise. It is not advisable to dispense with all ideas and purely focus on a single thread that would evolve into the final interpretation. At this stage, the brainstorming process should provide for some challenging and provocative answers to be considered. It is important to maintain freshness and originality even if the brief has a number of restrictions, such as a narrow target audience or seemingly 'uninteresting' subject matter. The application of creative processing by being inventive, imaginative and original is intrinsic and inherent to the individual. It is something that cannot be given, but can be brought out, controlled and directed. How much control and direction is down to the circumstance and situation of the illustrator at any given time. Certain briefs require total originality and a 'cutting edge' that can be contemporaneously 'on the edge'. In this sense it can be appropriate to go beyond expected and excepted boundaries. However, the imposed control of the illustrator's work – by tutor, art director, client – is in place to 'rein in' errant concepts and ideas. It is therefore better to be able to restrain the illustrator's inventiveness rather than have to 'push' for greater originality.

2

3 **4**

5

1–8. Mark Foreman has written and illustrated a children's book entitled 'Grandpa Jack's Tattoo Tales'. These images represent initial character development and concepts through to the finished illustrations.

6

7

8

'The application of creative processing by being inventive, imaginative and original is intrinsic and inherent to the individual. It is something that cannot be given, but can be brought out, controlled and directed.'

1

30 Completion

Evaluate the work produced at the initial stage and proceed with several ideas or concepts. Take risks with one or more, combine some and identify others that work disparately. Take these conceptions to a more finished state of visual complexity. The process of drawing will become a clear language of intent and meaning. Whether the imagery is to be imaginative or metaphorical, pictorially real or simplistic, visual clarity at this stage will facilitate the editing process and determine which solution to take towards completion.

Completion at this part of the process means the production of a finished visual. This happens after the approval of the chosen concept by evaluating the recently completed scamps (drawings produced to depict initial ideas).

A generalised definition of a visual is the presentation of a finished design or illustration solution for client approval before proceeding to finished artwork or final production. It should indicate clearly the subject matter and style of illustrative content, composition and colour, position of text, suggested typeface and placement of main headings or titles. It is often best rendered in a medium and style similar to that of the proposed image, although a detailed tonal pencil rendering can suffice if the intended imagery is realistically representational. If the intended outcome is a physically complex and interactive package, such as a book with 'pop-ups' and other engaging devices or features then a working dummy should be produced.

1–5. Nigel Owen's original thinking and conceptualisation show search and change regarding ideas, composition and content for this international airlines company advertising campaign. The initial processing and photographic research acquisition is shown sequentially within the sketchbook. The completed image manifests as a poster promoting travel to the UK. The client is United Airlines.

2

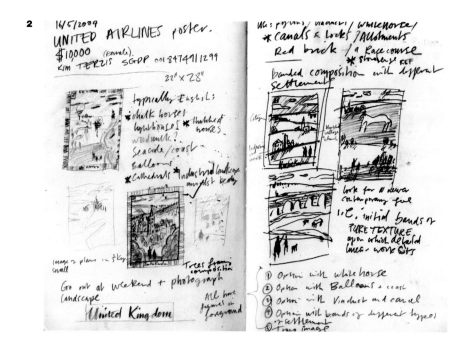

3

4

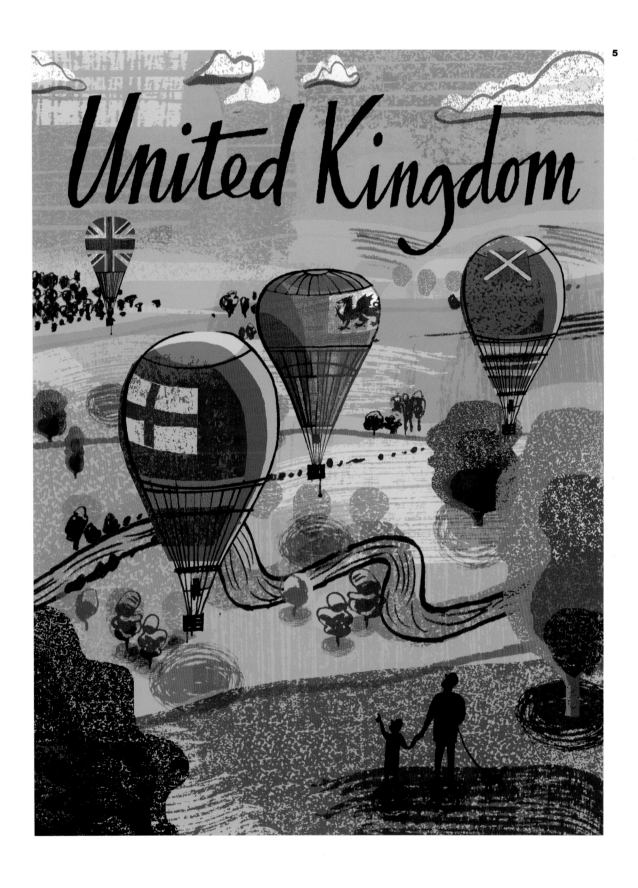

1

32 Research

The purpose of research in this context is in part to do with the straightforward acquisition of information for subject matter, but it can also be to demonstrate how the collation of data and the subsequent summary conclusions might make some appropriate contribution to knowledge. It does depend on the nature of the intended project and whether it is based in professional practice visual communication or is to be a visual thesis, both of which are defined and described in the section outlined in the rationale (see page 16). Whichever model appropriated at this level, research methodologies must be measured and testable against academic and intellectual need and firmly embedded into the project as exemplified by the objectives previously established.

This type of research is broadly described as 'Research *through* Art and Design'. It is applied research by practice in this instance, specifically that of drawing and illustration. It is a systematic enquiry that is directed towards the acquisition, conversion or extension of existing knowledge for use in particular applications. Examples might be the provision of material to be written about and illustrated by way of a published book or editorial article. It may be to do with the experimentation, analysis and dissemination of practical processes and visual language development and how that might facilitate new knowledge related to a specific cultural or scientific subject.

Research and Illustration

Philosophically, it can be argued that in the broad context of illustration practice, there is a distinct difference between **R**esearch and **r**esearch! The question has to be asked at the early stage of project development because it has a distinct bearing on outcomes and it is therefore important to ensure that the original aim of the brief is either adhered to or altered accordingly.

Research with a small **r** can be considered solely as the gathering of reference materials rather than 'research' proper, which has been

2

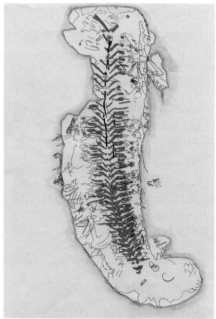

3

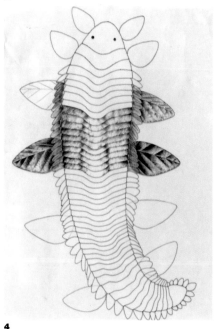

4

5

A sequence of four images representing significant stages in the development and completion of a research case study. The overall project, undertaken by the author, aims to present the creation and interpretation of new knowledge related to elements of evolution and palaeo-fauna.

1,2. This is the fossil of a hitherto unknown prehistoric organism.

3. A visual dissemination of anatomy.

4. The final drawing showing form, structure and visual ambience.

5. The original and first image ever produced of Keurbosia, an enigmatic marine invertebrate from 500 million years ago.

6

the subject of considerable debate in relation to art and design practice. Much illustration as we know is dependent on reference, even images of a fantastical and highly imaginative nature are underpinned or influenced by something that is real. However, if the need to succeed, whatever the brief and context of illustration might be, depends only on the acquisition of straightforward information – written, verbal and in many instances visual – the research outcomes still need to be firmly embedded directly into the finished imagery and evidenced by the content and quality of the visual communication.

Research in itself – with a capital **R** – is a distinct academic discipline. How might it and illustration come together? The notion of illustrators transcending the role of 'colouring-in technician' and assuming authority over content and subject matter takes on a whole new meaning regarding the application of research. In general, the illustration practice becomes much more holistic and assumes a certain gravitas regarding the rationale behind the intended work. Indeed, the research methodology is intrinsic with determining the rationale and aims of the intended work. The rationale, aims and objectives declare the criteria for the investigation against which the success or failure of the project can be assessed. It will also define the nature of the project and the main concerns of the investigation. This will guide the research.

Preparing for Research
The following questions are paramount regarding successful completion and must be considered before starting the work:

■ Would the project make an appropriate contribution to knowledge?
■ Can it be achieved by the methods described in the objectives?
■ Is it appropriate and timely to undertake a project of this nature now? Is the subject matter contemporaneous and/or generic with something that is 'cutting-edge' and would that have an impact that could either be positive or negative regarding the rationale?
■ Does one have the prior knowledge and the intellectual and practical skills to do this work? Is one's prior learning and experience a qualification to undertake this project and

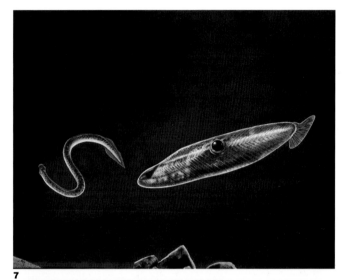

7

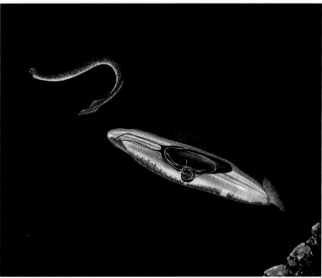

8

6,7,8. When conducting research, analyses and subsequent results will often require the presentation of more than one alternative theory or conclusion. Here, the author depicts two correlative images of an enigmatic aquatic organism from the Carboniferous period, each describing alternative physiology and physical orientation.

1a

34

is one's place on the learning curve sufficiently high enough?

■ What resources are needed? Does anyone specific need to supply them? Are materials, studio or other space appropriate and sufficient? Are specialist facilities and/or equipment required? Is there a need to temporarily relocate?

■ How much supervision, tutorial or specialist help is required?

■ What is the proposed time plan? Is there a confidence to complete by the deadline set?

If the aim is for a scholarly approach and the production of a visual thesis then it is important to set out the historical, contemporary and theoretical contexts. There should be an identification of the various strands of history that relates to the theme of the project. It may be a history of ideas and concepts that has influenced the subject matter being dealt with, the history of the media, materials or technology on which one proposes to work or a particular part of the history of illustration or visual communication.

It is also important to define the contemporary work that relates to the field of investigation. It should be done for the following reasons:

To demonstrate an awareness of the field of work.
To demonstrate that the proposed research will have some distinctiveness and be potentially original.
To form the basis of links with other research work to which there might be a contribution or building upon.

An element of theoretical context is important for every kind of project, though the degree of theoretical content will vary, particularly for practice-based visual work such as illustration. However, one should be able to demonstrate ways in which the work is evaluated and that of others, and the sources used to inform the evaluation.

A theoretical context will help avoid simply asserting a position and support a reflective approach needed for this higher level of study.

A sequence of four images from a research project by Serena Rodgers. This presents an enquiry into the processes involved for animators in creating new places and landscapes in their work through the internalisation and integration of the reality they observe, to the representation of the same on screen and to the creation of a new hyperreality.

1,1a. The first image reveals the progression of techniques where the figure is effectively drawn into the landscape.

2. The second shows an animated line within a box that acts as a character.

3. The third is a moving object that detracts from the landscape, but also acts as a figure.

4,4a. The fourth image depicts the figure stolen out of a landscape and replaced in a new setting, exposing the framing technique.

4a

Methodologies

The proposed methodologies or objectives as stated will provide an in-depth assessment of how effective and successful the project is and how the research has informed and facilitated its completion. It is therefore expedient to establish a project log that physically and appropriately would be a substantial sketchbook, able to contain all forms of visual work, such as drawings and photographs, and extracted printed elements, such as hard copy material from the internet and self-written work. As a matter of course, a review and understanding of the debates that surround the subject to be researched – historically and contemporaneously – should be presented in some form at the forefront of the log providing a solid platform for action.

The next stage of the project is to undertake an archival analysis. What is it that needs to be investigated? Break down the key elements of the enquiry and isolate them as individual tasks. Establish a programme of research through action with research methods identified. Outcomes related to these particular methods and tasks should be measured, timed and clearly described in the log.

Methods undertaken could be any of the following examples or a combination: library and database access, the Internet, fieldwork, studio work, interviews. Specific action may involve: correspondence by way of email, telephone, letter or face to face. Location reference gathering includes using written notes, drawing, taking photographs or live-action filming.

Initiative and innovation is important. It is essential to think around the problem and all the possible links associated with the subject being researched. Frequently certain actions deliver insufficient data and do not provide answers to the chief or key questions. One could go 'up a cul-de-sac' and not be able to proceed further with a particular line of enquiry. It may register the end of one aspect of research, but could also have a positive outcome and provide leads and new knowledge to subjects not previously considered, giving the project a new and striking twist.

3

4

1

36 Completion

The original aim of the project would have determined what outcomes should be expected at completion and whatever the key question or focus of investigation, the project should manifest predominately as visual material. This could be any or a combination of the following: finished illustrations within a visual communication context, finished illustrations that present new knowledge by way of primary research, experimental visual work and investigative drawing studies. The finished presentation could be part of or form examples of the following: books, published research papers, exhibition and/or interactive media packages such as CDs.

A summary account of the research data and findings should be fully recorded in the log. The project log is a very important part of the submission and it should contain throughout reflective and analytical association with the work undertaken. There should also be a written project report. The complexity and number of words should represent the original aim. The most scholarly form of practice-based project submission, the visual thesis, should contain a substantive amount of written work, the historical, contemporary and theoretical context, a full description of the methodologies undertaken with reflective and critical analysis, a detailed conclusion summarising the effectiveness of the research undertaken and what new or original knowledge there is to present. As an illustrator it is worth remembering that the notion of 'theorist-practitioner' has become a universal idea, particularly where the research is held within visual work. As far back as the Renaissance period, this was common practice; observe the way in which Leonardo da Vinci integrated pure scientific research with what can easily be classified as illustration practice. It can be stated with confidence that the visual language of illustration has, is and will continue to provide explanation, elucidation and clarity to many topics of research.

1–4. A research project entitled 'Speaking with the Sun' by Susan Boafo. This is a digital video production highlighting the relationship between aquatic algae, sunlight and the Earth's ecology. Each of the giant letters appearing in the video **2**, **3** & **4** is formed by the presence of thousands of microscopic, single-celled algae. Stencils for each letter were placed in front of jars containing the algae. The algae moved towards the light that passed through the stencils by a process called phototaxis, creating a new letter every 15 minutes. The letters (or algae) spell out the scientific formula for photosynthesis.
1. Imagery seen as a gallery exhibition installation (France 2006).

5,6. Eivind Bøvor's drawing of a character representation from the story 'Gormenghast'. This clearly demonstrates how drawing informs the illustrator's inherent visual language.

2

3

4

5

Drawing

Drawing is the principal faculty of illustration. It is the foundation on which visual imagery is built. It forms the basis of all styles of illustration, from representational realism to avant-garde abstraction. Every illustration has to be conceived, designed and rendered to completion and drawing plays a part in all of this.

Drawing also informs the illustrators' identity and develops and establishes one's personal iconography. It is the first functional attribute that an illustrator must acquire and determines the foundation of a visual vocabulary.

Observation and 'learning to see' is all part of the illustrator's education. A mastery of objective and analytical drawing will provide for detailed knowledge of subjects and will inform creativity and feed the imagination.

'We draw to understand our subject matter.'
James McMullin,
New York, September, 1996

In a practical sense, drawing constructs an image whether it is an imaginative illustration produced without visual reference, a geometrically designed diagram or an accurate pictorial reconstruction. Drawing deals with composition, colour and texture, shape, form, space and proportion, perspective, the emotive and associative aspects of subject matter and is a visual language of research and reference acquisition. Drawing is the way in which all visual ideas are externalised, from conception to completion.

1

38 **Objective and Analytical Development**

Objective and analytical drawing is the key to successful visual research and provides for a fundamental understanding and analysis of subject matter. It is a crucial academic and practical skill essential for illustrators when recording information and establishing concepts. Criteria for application will include elements that are fundamental to the accurate representation of subject matter. Most drawing of this kind is applied to the visual depiction or reconstruction of physical entities, but in order to achieve complete knowledge and understanding the drawing studies should determine the subjects' cultural and/or contemporary placing.

There are three key questions to be addressed and these can be applied to most objects, natural or man-made.

What?
'Morphology': form, structure, anatomy, how it is made.
Why?
'Ecology': where, when and with what?
How?
'Biology': how does or did it work, what does it do?

In order to satisfy these criteria, the working practice and process should be an extensive undertaking, particularly if the outcomes are for academic research purposes. The first objective is to synthesise data by gaining a working knowledge of the subject matter by the examination of the physical primary resource material – the actual object or specimen to be drawn – and if appropriate or convenient to collaborate with experts who might facilitate further reference gathering and provide in-depth information.

2. What? Form and structure:
A series of three black-and-white drawings by the author, commissioned to give archaeological identity to a palaeolithic axe head.

3. Why? Where, when and with what?:
This is a highly detailed visual reconstruction by the author depicting ecology and interaction within the South American rainforest.

4. How? How does it work, what does it do?: This extremely precise technical drawing provides ultimate reference regarding the engineering and workings of a traction engine.

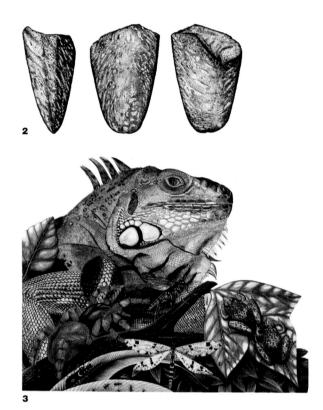

2

3

4

5

It is essential that a measured and calculated approach to rendering is applied and the inclusion of written notes is to be encouraged. A 'sketchy' and informal application to mark-making is inappropriate. Do not allow artistic licence to 'run amok', as visual disengagement with the aim would render the project invalid.

The visual language skills employed ought to range beyond the ability to render an attractive drawing based purely on surface mark-making. In addition to demonstrating a repertoire of techniques and artistic endeavours there has to be a defined understanding of the nature of the subject. The drawing should distinguish between important details and unnecessary anomalies, and utilise the most appropriate visual language to represent the subject matter faithfully. Drawing from the actual object provides a tangency with the subject. Observation and touch will facilitate an engagement with shape, form, surface texture, general ambience and physical presence. This analytical observation and visual scrutiny is a process of exploration and discovery leading to images of calculated exactitude. This method utilises a drawing strategy of search and change. Because there

6

5,6. Life class. Eivind Bøvor's figure drawing depicts accurate and visual scrutiny of the human form.

1,7–9. Tom Haskett's field studies of original Cornish tin mine buildings provide an excellent source of reference for the production of highly detailed architectural illustrations.

7

8

9

1

40

is a variety of ways of seeing, the same object can be seen and drawn in many ways, each just as 'real' and true as others.

These drawings make a visual statement about the observed object and should form a fundamental reference underpinning upon which illustration artwork can be completed, imagery that may be about explaining unseen workings and structures. The drawings should tell the truth succinctly and clearly about a chosen aspect. Good objective drawings of this nature are selective and single minded.

Whether or not one is engaged in a specific project that requires drawing for research or reference gathering purposes, students and professional illustrators should regularly undertake to do objective drawing, over and above anything else. It is inimical to neglect the discipline of drawing from life.

Attend either regular life sessions or simply draw anything appropriate that is around at any given time. Understanding human anatomy and being able to accurately represent the figure will give scope for a breadth of applications to illustration. It is a common misconception that objective and academic drawing leads solely to 'realistic' illustration. The truth will suggest that excellent drawing skills will facilitate experimentation and the knowledge gained will feed the imagination with images that can later find their way into more creative work.

2

1–4. Life class. Gary Long demonstrates, through these drawings, an observed and accurate recording of anatomical form and structure along with an aesthetic adherence to the quality of line and mark-marking.

'Understanding human anatomy and being able to accurately represent the figure will give scope for a breadth of applications to illustration.'

3

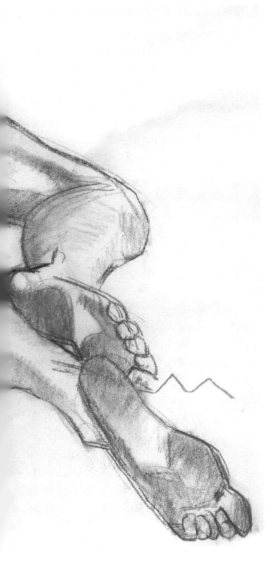

4

1

42 **Visual Note Taking**

The sketchbook is an all important tool for
illustrators. It is where the action of visual
note taking manifests and where the process
of developing one's visual vocabulary begins.
The sketchbook will function for the initial
stages of ideas development for visual
communication and will provide a place for
personal and observational studies. The
conveyance and utilisation of a sketchbook,
constantly and routinely, is important for
one's perception of the immediate
environment and should be encouraged for
use in any situation, formal or informal.

The most common practice of visual note
taking is to draw on location and document
or record elements of interest that could be
used as reference at a later stage or to
specifically target subjects required by a
given brief. Either could appear as
'reportage' illustration, imagery used in
published form that was actually produced
on site, usually in the sketchbook.

2

3

4

5

1–5. These full-colour
gouache studies by
Gary Long are visual
preparations for a series
of larger images based
on the theme of slate
quarrying in New
England. Composition,
the use of colour, light
and general ambience
and atmosphere are all
important elements
being considered.

6–9. A series of
reportage drawings by
Mark Foreman
produced in a
sketchbook on location
in New York, they
record and document
characters and scenes
related to Manhattan
life.

10. A pack of blank
playing cards provided
Mark Foreman with the
opportunity to produce
location drawings of
New York in an
innovative and novel
way.

6

Examples can be extremely varied both in subject matter and contextual use. The following is typical; a journalistic style commentary of a particular event anywhere in the world, stylistically narrative and providing a 'hands-on' record of atmosphere and sense of place. This is broadly generic and provides a very general description. It may be that specifics are inherent in the imagery, such as a capturing of certain aspects of everyday life with people of all descriptions interacting in some way. In this instance it may be important to visually record aspects of gesture, movement and body language, dynamics and scale with all elements depicted within the setting of their time and place.

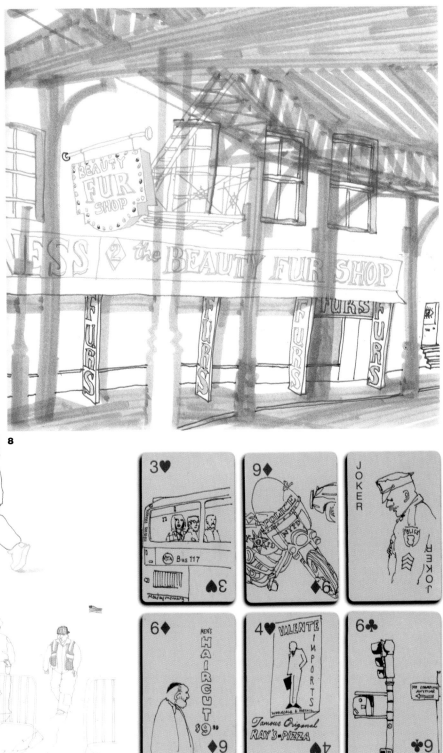

8

7

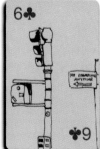

9

10

1

44 Observational drawings of this nature can be less formal regarding visual language, particularly when compared to the detailed scrutiny of subject matter required of pure academic objective drawing. A 'looser' and more economic approach to mark-making will enable the associative and atmospheric nature of what one is visually recording to be a priority. Creative and ambient approaches can be developed. This way of working can often record the 'soul' and influence of a subject or location, and goes beyond documenting surface features. It also goes beyond the 'cold' visual representation of people and there can start to be a capturing of human emotion, mood, character and personality.

2

3

4

5

1–5. A trip to Manhattan has given Tom Haskett favourable occasion to visually record details of many aspects related to life in New York. These drawings can be used as a source of reference at a later stage.

6–9. Pages from Nigel Owen's sketchbook reveal the creative and conceptual processes that manifest as initial drawings and notes related to solving problems of visual communication. This is a commission to produce an illustrated map of Andalusia for promotional purposes.

6

Externalisation of Ideas and Freedom of Expression

This process is specific to the start of solving problems of visual communication. The 'real' answering of the brief begins here. As when engaged in the process of visual note taking, the place for this activity will be the sketchbook. The drawings produced should not be inhibited by vagaries of technical accuracy or realism. The idea or concept is paramount. It can be supposed that one's 'style' is already established and that the form and way of the illustration(s), for whatever the context or concept the brief requires, would already be assumed. It is also expedient to dispense with any notion of creating aesthetic 'masterpieces' in the sketchbook. Maybe the finished illustration artworks should be so, but the methods adopted ought to allow for complete creative and imaginative freedom and the concept of 'doodling' is to be encouraged. One could conceive a multitude of concepts and visual proposals this way, from initial sequencing or storyboarding for books and animations, complex diagrams or information systems, to developing characters or other such principal entities for storytelling, editorial or promotional purposes.

It is often the case that one is required to create an image without the subject being present. There may be several ways to proceed:

■ Notebook and/or sketchbook referencing. The process of brainstorming and visual note taking could provide a solid starting point.
■ The recollection of anecdotal detail related to domestic or everyday occurrences. There may also be something specific or significant that one has experienced.
■ The recollection of information related to 'cosmopolitan' or professional experiences, such as international visits or specific research undertakings.

By carrying a sketchbook at all times, inspiration can occur anywhere and in the unlikeliest of places. Wherever one is engaged in creating ideas, on location or in the studio, by using a 'loose' and informal method of sketching – 'doodling' – immediate visual statements can be made. If the requirement is for a pictorial

7

8

9

1

46 representation of people interacting in some way, then draw as 'matchstick' figures, creating whatever concept is appropriate, erasing, changing and adapting at will. Think in terms of creating drama; what if one was directing live action for films and allow total freedom of expression when drawing. Avoid clamming-up and not moving forward from the initial ideas.

By not having the constraints of overly specific details and references to draw from, one's imagination is free to create literally anything. If the brief requires such an approach then the illustrator can 'go anywhere' and 'do anything'. To a degree, this can be classed as 'letting go of control'. Ambient, decorative, metaphorical and fantastical images can be innovated and conceived at this stage by using whatever visual means appropriate – colour, texture or line. It could represent the merging of reality with fantasy whereby any combination of approaches can be used; drawing from memory, from references or from pure imagination.

2

3

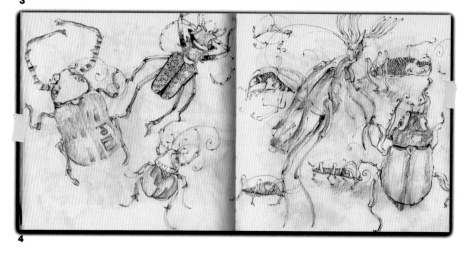

4

2–4. Creative processing and the externalisation of ideas are solidly prevalent in Katherine Child's sketchbook. These pages represent initial inspiration and thoughts, which were later developed into the layouts of double-page spreads for a book.

1,5–11. This sequence of drawings by Nigel Owen depicts initial 'doodling' processes and an uninhibited freedom of representation for themes and subjects. Ideas and concepts are initiated and discarded until the requirements of the brief are fully met. In this instance the overall design is for a book cover and includes image and titling.

5

6

7

8

9

10

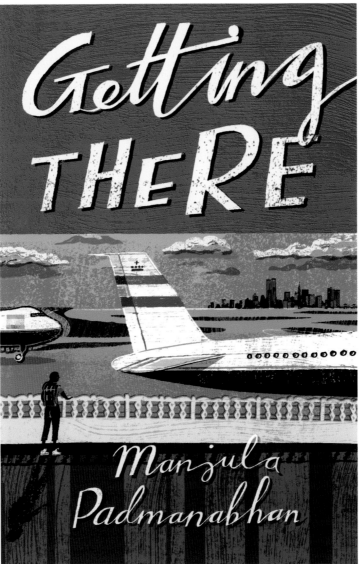

11

2

The Nature of Imagery

'It is the distinctive visual language
that identifies one's 'mark' or personal
iconography.'

Visual Language
Stylisation
Visual Intelligence

Visual Metaphor
Conceptual Imagery and Surrealism
Diagrams
Abstraction

Pictorial Truths
An Overview of Literal Representation
Hyperrealism
Stylised Realism
Sequential Imagery

Aesthetics and Non-Aesthetics
Trends
'Chocolate Box'
'Shock'

1

2

Visual Language

Stylisation

The majority of practising professional illustrators, along with many graduating or convocational student illustrators will have a 'style' associated with their work.

What is meant by style? It is the distinctive visual language that identifies one's 'mark' or personal iconography. It is that particular feature or quality that determines what kind of illustration one is associated with. It should also define one's placement within a visual, illustration genre. Like music, literature and fine art, an applied art and design discipline such as illustration will comprise numerous variations, themes and treatments. Some will represent an adherence to a contemporary trend or fashion and others will be more traditional.

A historical and contemporary overview of illustration will depict seemingly hundreds of styles. However, in broad terms, there are just **two** forms of imagery. All variations of visual language will be placed within one of these. *Literal* illustrations tend to represent pictorial truths. Here there is generally an accurate description of reality and even if the image

'It is the distinctive visual language that identifies one's "mark" or personal iconography.'

1,2. Far from any pretence of pictorial reality this conceptual image by David Bain presents a visual interpretation of the quote: 'there was once a game, which a sharper played with a dupe, entitled, "Heads I Win, Tails You Lose"'.

3. John Aggs has utilised the conceptual process to determine a final image that exemplifies the quote: 'Normally, I read my classics in strip form' (Tommy Steele).

4. Richard Duckett's highly realistic and precisely crafted rendition of a helicopter is an excellent example of literal realism.

3

depicts narrative fiction of a fantastical or dramatic nature, the accent is on creating a scene that is credible. Examples of visual language can vary from hyperrealism rendered digitally or by traditional drawing methods to painterly, impressionistic or decorative approaches. Objective and pictorial representation falls within this category. The second form of illustration can be described as *conceptual*. Here we can have metaphorical applications to the subject or visual depictions of ideas or theories. The images may contain elements of reality, but as a whole take a different form of being. Examples may include diagrams, composites, surrealism, extreme distortion or abstraction.

Both forms of illustration can be applied to all five contexts of practise; **information, commentary, narrative fiction, persuasion, identity**. However, some styles are best suited to specific or particular uses. Examples might be where hyperrealism is the most appropriate visual language to convey detailed information, caricature and distortion to represent political satire and the imaginative juxtaposition of visual elements to present an entertaining image for advertising purposes.

It can broadly be agreed upon that such is the versatility of illustration regarding the breadth of visual language that as an applied art form it can depict anything and in any style. However, it is important to regard that stylisation has to be appropriate for the subject matter, the context of operation and ensure a considered receptivity for the audience. Illustration practise is individualistic regarding visual language and there can be far reaching and challenging aspects to one's style, often to the point of utilising more than one.

However, it is interesting to note that in the business and professional practise environment, many illustrators' representatives or agents will insist on promoting one style, preferring to 'pigeon-hole' individuals claiming that it is easier to promote and sell an illustrator's work this way. Many publishers and other clients take the opposite view and prefer to commission and work with an illustrator who is able to work with a variety of styles.

4

1

52   Visual Intelligence

Analysing the concept of visual language cannot be carried out comprehensively without due consideration to the notion of visual intelligence. This can also be posed along with another consideration; what makes for a successful visual image?

Answers might reveal the following; aesthetic judgement, 'taste', the emotive use of colour, texture and shape, and symbolism. All of this points to human subjectivity and personal preferences. However, illustration is broadly objective. Contextually speaking, in order to measure the quality of the image one must consider how successful the transfer of messages has been. As previously stated, an image without a context is not illustration. Nonetheless, emotive reaction and response is paramount in certain circumstances. A non aesthetic or 'bad taste' approach may be required when the aim is to shock, present a contentious argument or even depict unsavoury material for educational purposes.

It is not appropriate to dwell on technique or the vagaries of mark-making. However, an individual visual language is, in some part, determined by this. An illustrator whose style relies upon spontaneous and aggressive autography can give an image the 'fire' required to invoke audience reaction. Alternatively, sensitive and highly meticulous painting may provide the detail and aesthetic qualities appropriate for an

informative illustration of a natural history subject.

Return to the idea of visual intelligence. A naively produced illustration may suggest a lack of visual intelligence; poor drawing, inappropriate choices made regarding colour, composition, pictorial or conceptual elements and subjects. There also seems to be a certain ambiguity when visual intelligence is recognised and associated with an image. Perhaps it can be seen as an identifiable maturity; experience, visual sophistication and contextual understanding are all important criteria to consider when making these judgements.

1,2. Arthur de Borman's illustration for a book of 'Trivia' combines humour with a clearly defined visual language thus giving this style a particular identity. The use of visual intelligence is apparent by way of the distorted figure representation and the linear markings to convey 'pognophobia is the fear of beards'.

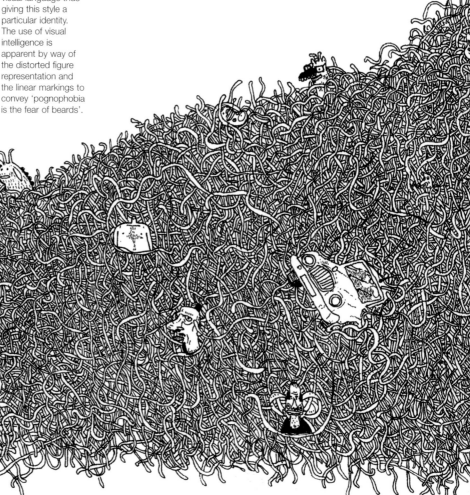

1

54   Visual Metaphor

Conceptual Imagery and Surrealism

A generalised definition of a visual metaphor
might suggest the description of an image
that is imaginative, but not literally
applicable. When applied to the discipline of
illustration, it is commonplace to describe
this form of imagery as being conceptual.
This implies a way of depicting content by
utilising a number of ideas and methods
of communication, illusion, symbolism,
and expressionism.

This type of visual stylisation started to
evolve during the 1950s in the United States
when issues and themes, as publicised in
magazines, were becoming more critical and
complex. There seemed a need to present the
viewer with much more enigmatic and
ambiguous images that invited deeper
interpretation. Up to this period, illustration
was more or less completely dominated by
explicitly literal and vividly realistic drawing
and painting. The chief exponent was
Norman Rockwell who had himself derived
his style from early proponents of American
commercial illustration; J.D. Layendecker,
N.C. Wyeth, et al.

However, whilst this particular visual
language is still successful and appropriate for
dramatic reconstructions across all contexts
of illustration practice, the need to express
ideas rather than portray verbatim scenes has
meant that conceptual illustration is now the
dominant style.

Historically, photography replaced much of
the figurative realism used in advertising.
Today, it is photography and not drawing
that dominates the pages of magazines and
roadside billboards. However, this has
presented illustrators with a much more
challenging role; to be both interpretative
and to convey the 'texture' of a topic or idea
rather than, like photography, present just the
'veneer' or 'surface' of the subject.

What exactly is the visual language of
conceptual illustration and broadly speaking
what does it look like? This question cannot
be answered fully by merely presenting a
singular succinct definition. One has to
examine firstly the modern art painting

2

3

1,2. Richard Borge's
overtly conceptual
image presents an
unambiguous
comment regarding
the state of
'censorship'.

3. The illustrator Brad
Holland is renowned
for conceiving and
producing striking
visual concepts for a
range of contextual
uses. This conceptual
image is to promote a
production entitled
'Red' by the Wharf
Theatre Co. The visual
message conveys a
comment on the effect
the Communist
Revolution and Red
Guard had on traditional
Chinese theatre.

4. David Ho produces
an uncompromisingly
surreal image entitled
'The Way'.

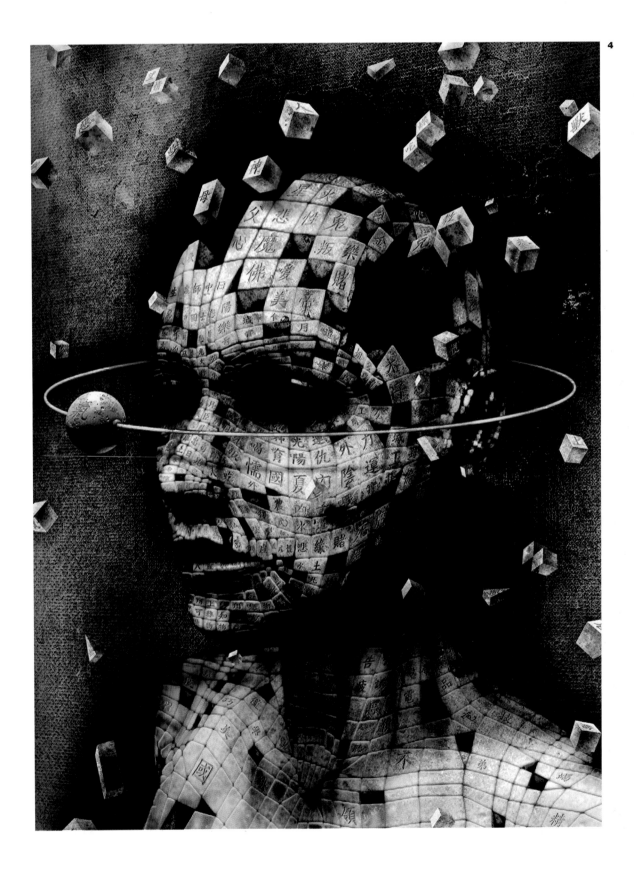

56

movements and styles that have influenced the progress of conceptual illustration and secondly view the work of illustrators, both historically and contemporaneously who have been successful proponents of this genre.

Surrealism, abstract expressionism and cubism have provided illustrators with immeasurable influence regarding the nature of imagery, exemplified by the expressive application of colour and form that marries elements of realism with abstraction. There is also distortion and juxtaposition of compositional elements to create illusory and dreamlike interpretations presenting enigmatic and thought-provoking commentaries, identities and promotions.

Examine the biggest influence on conceptual illustration: surrealism. Réne Magritte, the Belgian surrealist painter has had a considerable influence on early conceptual illustration. Unlike Salvador Dali, whose paintings were often rooted in interpreting subconscious fantasies, Magritte presented a clearer, though enigmatic, symbolic visual language that illustrators found could be applied to contemporary themes and issues as commissioned by the commercial marketplace; a euphonium and other bizarre objects floating in space, a sky where the clouds have turned into French loaves, a train coming through a fireplace, a rain shower of bowler-hatted men.

These concepts have obviously and unashamedly borne some influence on illustrations that have been commissioned from the 1950s to the present day: businessmen climbing ladders up to the clouds; two men with one eye sharing the same pair of spectacles; twigs, leaves and flowers growing from the fingers of an outstretched hand. Clichéd, yes, and the list of examples is almost infinite. These types of illustrations have been and are to this day being commissioned to promote, comment and give identity to issues related to the economy, politics and society. Commonplace themes manifested by way of published editorials, company literature and promotional material.

1,2. Etienne Delessert provides surreal portraits of Dracula and King Arthur.

3. Wilson McLean's editorial illustration for 'Penthouse' uses typical principles of surrealism with scenic distortion and disregard for the conventional representation of 'real space'. There is also an unnerving juxtaposition of visual elements.

4,5. Victoria Rose uses collage to design and construct this conceptual editorial illustration entitled 'No More Coins'.

6. Arthur de Borman has produced an image promoting a motion picture about a man who saves many Jews from death and persecution in Nazi Germany.

4

Conceptual illustration has been viewed as an element of the design process and it is the illustrator, not usually the commissioning art director who originates and defines the totality of the image and its graphic positioning, whether a poster, cover of a company report or double-page spread in a book. This often means the illustrator giving due consideration and application to the inclusion and placement of typographic and other visual devices and elements. The whole conceptual image – in other words the complete illustrations – as seen in its complete graphic totality is the work of the illustrator.

In previous times and to a certain extent today, the art director will position the image near or amongst the appropriate text. But it is the illustrator who translates the verbal ideas into visual ones, including the smaller 'spot' illustrations as seen in magazines and newspapers.

To quote the art director Steven Heller: 'Conceptual illustration serves two purposes: It provides meaning – and commentary – and gives a publication its visual personality.'

Conceptual illustrators to be aware of include the following: Marshall Arisman, Brad Holland, Alan E. Cober and Anita Kunz. All have been or are on the cutting edge of this genre: award winning, influential, professionally and commercially successful. An analysis of their work will reveal a challenge to the accepted way in which people see and think. Stylistically different from one another – in use of media and iconography – their work can be seen as a standard-bearer.

To conclude, the visual imagery that is conceptual illustration does not rely on the appearance of being true or the semblance of actuality. It questions the concepts of definition and representation and will continue to evolve and grow with the demands and vicissitudes of society.

5

6

1

58 Diagrams

What defines a diagram? It is usually an illustration that depicts the features of an object, a system, a manufactured or organic process by way of an exposition that goes far from pictorial reality. The visual language can comprise graphical or symbolic representation and contextually does not work unless the information or message is clearly elucidated.

We normally associate diagrams with educational textbooks: black-and-white line drawings with simple annotation accompanying technical, academic literature. The overall ambience of these publications was, and to a certain extent is, 'dry', overtly scholarly and overly formal. But in a contemporary sense, one can apply the term diagram to an array of innovative and richly colourful images that go way beyond the basics of pure information graphics; illustrated maps, detailed cross sections, engaging interactive features that not only facilitate an educative need, but can also provide an appropriate visual alternative for use in advertising campaigns, for promotional purposes or for editorial commentaries.

But what actually distinguishes a diagram from any other form of illustration and what is it that defines its nature as a visual language? Within the context of this book it is positioned with visual metaphor. However, the original raison d'être of a diagram is to communicate information. Therefore, one would assume that truth and reality would be paramount to its intention and to a large extent that is a fundamental concern to the content of the diagram.

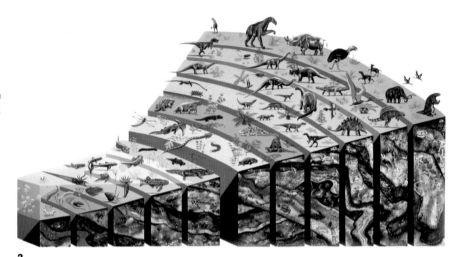

2

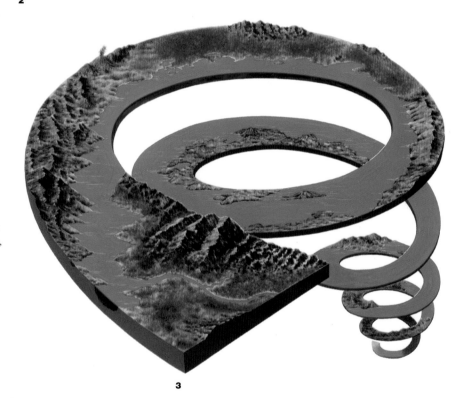

3

1,5. The illustrated map is an example of how such a graphic representation can diagrammatically convey appropriate information. Here, Nigel Owen's 'Whiskies of Scotland' is also used in a promotional context.

2,3. The author has produced alternative diagrammatic concepts of the same theme: a geologic timeline of the Earth.

4,6. Highly detailed and illustrative cross sections often provide ideal visual concepts to convey very specific scientific information. Martin Macrae depicts the ecology and composition of soil in a way photography or actual realism could not.

4

But often, the specific aspects of concerns related to subject matter cannot be conveyed by realistic or pictorial means alone. Complex processes and systems, technical or scientific data, composite structures and physical features, instructions and descriptions all suggest an approach that demands conceptuality. However, this does not mean producing an image that is either surreal or not literally applicable to the subject. It may be expedient to consider terms that apply to certain types of diagram. This could suggest, in a visual sense, some of the differentials: chart, graph, table, cladogram, map. These descriptions imply the visual stylisation and underpinning upon which all diagrams, including the most innovative and contemporary would have to conform.

The symbolism and graphic devices, the juxtaposition of free-standing representational elements and/or abstract components will vary considerably from diagram to diagram. As will the subject matter. However, such is the need to impart information and provide visual description – whatever the contextual requirements might be and whatever the media from print, website or moving image – that the role and status of the diagram will increase.

5

6

1

60   Abstraction

The term 'abstract' has become synonymous with a number of 20th-century art movements: abstract expressionism, cubism, constructivism, neo plasticism to name but a few. Borne out of a need to counteract the sabotaging of pictorial, figurative imagery by photography, painters engaged in a practice that bore no relation to nature or reality. They basically worked with colours and shapes of their own invention. This assertion can also be associated with illustrators whose visual language could be described as abstract; stylistically abstruse and unpictorial, free from representation.

Commercial artists have been using this type of imagery since the advent of full-colour printing. However, it has been considered as within the working domain of the graphic designer because in a historical context illustrators were concerned purely with the production of pictorial representation. Posters, book covers, point-of-sale material, packaging and promotional literature have been subjected to either decorative, expressive or atmospheric approaches, usually with accompanying type and titling that can sometimes be integrated as part of the imagery. Often produced by way of a collage technique, the overall concept may comprise flat colours that could be 'subtle' and/or 'loud', textures, shapes that could be informal and/or geometrically formal, free-floating elements that are not anchored to any pictorial reality. Today, this particular trend in image conception and creation is firmly embedded within the discipline of contemporary illustration.

1,2. David Lesh utilises a distinct visual language that is both abstract and conceptual. These two images fall within the contextual domain of identity and are corporate in suggestion.

3–5. Joel Nakamura's imagery comprises elements of symbolism and ethnicity.

6. Alana Roth has a contemporary style that is uninhibited regarding notions of visual distortion and abstraction.

7. Jessica Allen has combined decorative yet symbolic representation within an appropriately evocative, colourful and textural abstract composition. The image accompanies a text from 'A Walk with a White Bushman' by Laurens van der Post.

2

3

4

5

It is often within this domain of visual imagery that illustrators embark upon attempts to 'break new ground'. This may be no more than a superficial adherence to the notion that illustration has to 'move forward'. But let us return to the fact that the best illustrations are those that not only adhere to the brief set, but communicate effectively and creatively through the context prescribed. Perhaps 'moving forward' should be more to do with contemporaneous content and subject matter rather than trying to push the boundaries of mark-making.

In recent years the boundaries of visual language were broken, more by chance than by experimentation. The digital revolution has seen to it. 'Slick', computer-enhanced or produced composites of formal or bought photographic and/or autographic imagery, give rise to a new form of visual corporate and promotional material, replete with contemporary 'state of the art' themes and subjects, manipulated and 'super airbrushed' to new heights of 'shininess' and 'slickdom'.

This has taken abstract and conceptual illustration to a new domain. But has it reached its zenith, both in terms of popularity and trend? It certainly does not provide the illustrator who creates these images with much visual identity. Personal iconography, one's own particular 'mark', is confined to a genre of generalised 'computer graphics' or 'digital arts'. However, as a conclusion, it must be said that abstract illustration and other forms of conceptual imagery have in recent years greatly expanded the parameters of the discipline. It is one of the reasons why there has been both a blurring and shifting of boundaries within the visual arts and communication disciplines. Illustrators not only conceive ideas, but design complete concepts such as posters and book jackets – no longer the exclusive domain of the graphic designer. Illustrators use and produce photographic imagery. All of this points to a leading question. Where and what will constitute the discipline of illustration in both the near and distant future?

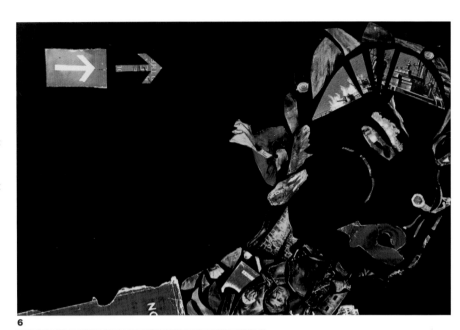

6

7

'Abstract: stylistically abstruse and unpictorial, free from representation.'

1

62 Pictorial Truths

An Overview of Literal Representation
Historically, all illustration fell into the category of literal representation. This also applies to what we might broadly and generally describe as 'art'. Prior to the advent of the camera, this was the only form of imagery to be found whatever the genre or period being examined. We are dealing with imagery that is largely produced to convey reality without an overemphasis on conceptual mysticism, allegory or metaphor.

Prehistoric art provided vivid, lifelike images of animals and humans, found incised, painted or sculpted on the walls deep inside the caves where our ancestors sheltered. The Ancient Egyptians created clear, scenic representations of human forms in their idealised prime with families, servants, objects, animals and food. Roman mosaics, although principally decorative were often given to portraying scenes of daily life.

In later times, the Renaissance period introduced the first considered representations of perspective and architectural accuracy. Scientific discoveries and technological advancements also provided much material for the likes of Leonardo da Vinci to 'illustrate' realistic anatomical details and notions of aerodynamics. Indeed, during much of this period and subsequent periods, the 'art' in question is firmly embedded in the suggestions that define the description of illustration; commissioned imagery, often at the behest of the church, state or wealthy benefactors from Michelangelo's frescos to the figurative landscapes and portrait artists of the 19th century.

What is meant by literal representation in the context of both historical and contemporary illustration? It may be expedient to attach another description – pictorial realism: in other words the drawing and painting of 'pictures' whatever the contextual use or subject matter.

In this sense a picture is the representation of a place, however large or small, with whatever components necessary, such as people or other objects, positioned or

2

'Pictorial realism: in other words the drawing and painting of "pictures" whatever the contextual use or subject matter.'

1,2. Roger Harris recreates an unnervingly realistic and frightening scenario.

3,5. Joanne Glover utilises the standard precept of three visual planes of scenic image construction within this highly detailed exposé of invertebrate life amongst the spring flowers: close foreground, middle ground and infinite plane.

4. A literal, visual representation should, when appropriate, accurately convey perspective and a credible notion of 'real space' with all elements focused and detailed accordingly. Martin Macrae's rainforest vista is an excellent example.

3

interacting in a visually credible way. There
would be a certain amount of concern for
accuracy regarding elements of perspective
space and scale. However, that is not to say
that deliberate distortion and a 'bending of
the truth' does not take place. Many historic
and contemporary books of children's
narrative fiction, particularly for very young
readers are described as 'picture books'.
Fantastical and magical scenes are conjured
up with people, animals or aliens with wildly
exaggerated, comical and/or caricatured
features. But these images do conform
generally to the concept of 'picture'. They
are fundamentally scenic with all
components physically 'working properly'
and interacting in a convincing manner. All
contexts of illustration practice use literal
representation. It can be seen everywhere:
on packaging such as book jackets, in
advertising such as posters and hoardings, in
non-fiction material such as encyclopaedias
and reference books. It is used in all forms of
narrative fiction, the pictorial qualities ideal
to create dramatic effect particularly when
used in sequence, such as graphic novels and
comic strips.

Stylistically, the visual language of literal
representation can vary greatly. It is true that
the majority conforms to accurate
representation, but the iconography and
subsequent autography can be as varied as
those described under the banner of
visual metaphor with photorealism and
impressionism to name but a few.

But by whichever means the imagery is
conceived and produced, there are generally
just two different visual languages employed:
linear and tonal. Linear illustration uses the
drawn line, however informal or formal and
whatever weight and variety to convey all
the major aspects of the image from outline
shapes, perspective and structure, to elements
of tone and highly detailed features. This
is not to describe a black-and-white
illustration. The vast majority of linear
illustrations are in full-colour. The colour is
often applied in either a loose textural,
vignetted, informal way or opaquely flat.
Whichever, the colour does not conflict or
interfere with the line nor is it used to
define any particular feature, either of the
scene in general or of the components.

4

5

64 A tonal illustration can be more 'realistic' and perhaps more accurately representational. This is because the image – whatever means used to render either traditional, impressionistic painting techniques to quasi 'airbrushed' digital – is made by tonal effect. Tone and where appropriate colour, is used to define all aspects of the image and consequently manifests as realism.

To conclude, the breadth of visual language and application given to literal representation can provide a sense of reality with some value-added aesthetics, invention and imagination.

Hyperrealism

Throughout history, artists have recreated pictorial compositions that strive for intense detail and reality. The subject matter has been exceptionally diverse, from depicting scenes of daily life, the glorification of regal or political leaders, religious and other cultural subjects, including narrative prose and verse. As time progressed there became a clearer and more applied understanding of visual representation from the use of perspective, scale and proportion to that indefinable ability to bring the subject 'to life': the sparkle in the eye, the realistic gestures and simulation of movement giving credibility to the image. This was all borne out of painstaking observation and a masterful handling of media and technique.

During the 19th century, certain members of the Pre-Raphaelite Brotherhood created images of great and florid detail and were amongst the first artists to achieve such striking realism by using the medium of brush and oil paint on canvas. Examples are 'April Love' by Arthur Hughes, 'Ophelia' by John Everett Millais and the 'Hireling Shepherd' by William Holman Hunt. This type of painting set a precedent for 20th-century hyperrealistic art and illustration. In the United States, the so-called 'sentimentalists', such as the artist/illustrator Winslow Homer painted hyperreal scenes of North American life, particularly themes related to Native Americans. Imagery of this nature dominated the domain of commercial illustration up until the 1950s and could be seen embedded within all aspects of publishing and advertising.

1,2. An illustration by Lorena Pugh entitled 'Innocence' contains a slight element of surreality yet is overtly hyperreal in essence. Rendered traditionally in oil on linen it comprises the best principles of draughtsmanship with all pictorial elements remaining in focus.

3. The requirement to advertise a certain brand of wine has initiated the conception of this highly technical yet evocative image by Richard Duckett.

4. This portrait of the musician Jimmy Rushing by Gary Cooley assumes an almost photographic quality regarding tonal values, but the underlying painterly quality provides a distinct aestheticism.

5

But how does hyperrealistic imagery relate to the contemporary world of illustration and how would one actually describe it as a visual language? Must it be argued that the best quality, untampered photograph captures reality best? After all, 'the camera never lies'!

However, an image that represents a literal, pictorial truth, but is classed as illustration goes beyond the traditional photographic picture in terms of its inherent being as a visual language. For example, a traditionally rendered image can, by its very 'physicality', in other words by way of subtle use of tone, texture and colour and by the opacity of the medium, create atmosphere and drama accompanied by meticulous details. Equally as important is the fact that one's own style and iconography can be revealed in an image such as this. Other aspects to consider when defining the nature of hyperreal illustration is that although an overall image may be seemingly 'photographic', contextual requirements such as a need for the depiction of intense detail throughout will suggest that every corner and component of the composition is rendered in sharp focus.

Often, scenic interpretations for information, advertising or narrative fictional purposes will be formed by way of combining three visual planes: the immediate foreground, depicting a few inches/centimetres to about six feet/two metres distance from the eye, the middle ground and beyond that, the infinite plane.

Every aspect rendered in hyper detail with no blurred effects simulates photographic imagery. Indeed, the very purpose of most hyperrealistic illustration is to recreate an image that cannot be produced photographically.

The following provide typical examples of this genre:

A natural science-based image for information purposes with a composite scene of a defined ecosystem comprising corresponding and appropriate fauna placed within their environment.

An image for narrative fiction or for historical information purposes that is

6

7

5–7. Gary Long's autographically rendered figure illustrations exemplify the visual language of hyperreality with a hint of the painterly. These images were produced to advertise a natural remedy for calmness in the face of life's daily pressures.

1

66 a dramatic and atmospheric reconstruction with intense interaction between characters. A well known example here is an illustration created by the late Tom Lovell depicting the surrender of General Robert E Lee to the Commander of the Union forces at the end of the American Civil War.

An advertising image that comprises 'delicious' fruits and other delicacies for human consumption arranged as a still life.

Creating dramatic and atmospheric effect is more straightforward for the illustrator than the photographer. One has the facility to adapt colours, textures and compositional elements to suit whatever purpose. As a visual language the aim is to make the subject in question look 'real' even if it is not. The digital age has provided illustrators with the means to transform imagery completely and out of all original recognition. Much of what is considered hyperrealistic illustration in a contemporary sense has been produced almost entirely by using digital means.

It is also possible to combine photographic imagery with traditional autography as exemplified by the British illustrator Larry Rostant who works within the domain of hyperrealism and creates characters and scenarios for all contextual purposes, including motion pictures.

Practitioners of this genre today have been criticised for not 'moving forward' in terms of style and innovation. It can be said in defence of hyperrealism that it must be judged in the same objective manner as all forms of illustration. Does it creatively and conceptually convey the message it is conceived for convincingly and appropriately to its target audience?

2

3

'A traditionally-rendered image can create atmosphere and drama, accompanied by meticulous details.'

1,4. Andrew Hutchinson takes hyperrealism to heights of immaculate detail with this natural history portrait.

2. Technological subjects are often best suited to hyperrealistic treatment and stylisation; a 'Stealth' fighter aircraft by John Fox.

3. The author has produced an image considered hyperreal, but rendered in black-and-white line and stipple. This is for an editorial entitled 'The Lost Children of Afghanistan'.

5. Gary Long has produced a promotional illustration entitled 'Tribute to Rockwell', emulating excellent pictorial, compositional and human figure representation.

4

5

1

68 Stylised Realism

What is stylised realism and how does one define it both historically and in a contemporary sense? Perhaps art history can elucidate some imagery that has influenced illustrators to produce work that could be considered realistic and not?

With the exception of iconic or decorative imagery from early times, one of the first movements to deliberately shift from pure realistic representation was impressionism. This particular style has had much influence on pictorial-based illustrators who work in a painterly fashion. Originally, impressionist painters such as Monet celebrated the overwhelming vision of nature seen in the splendour of natural light – whether dawn, daylight or twilight. They were fascinated by the relationships between light and colour and rendered paint informally and loosely, often using pure pigments only.

Another movement from the early 20th century is expressionism, which employed similar technical approaches but embedded within it a completely different rationale. Here, the proponents of this movement such as Oskar Kokoschka sought to develop pictorial forms which would express innermost feelings rather than represent the outside world. They employed exaggeration, distorted and vivid colours rendered with a vigorous and restless energy. This form of image-making, which employs such described effects and painterly treatments has been and can be seen throughout all contexts of illustration practice. Examples can include pastiche imagery emulating thus described art movements to advertise or narrate. There is also children's narrative fiction and an appropriate example is the book entitled 'The Whales' Song', illustrated by Gary Blythe. Also, packaging such as wine labels will use this type of impressionistic visual language providing ambience and attraction for said products.

2

3

4

5

1,5. Jonathan Burton utilises two distinct visual languages where both could be considered as containing elements of reality and yet are distinctly stylised. The scenario with the car is slickly 'airbrushed' – albeit digitally – whilst the figure with Stalin is appropriately distorted to convey personality and concern.

2,6. Levi Pinfold's narrative illustration for a self-written science-fiction story creates a pictorially convincing and credible scene, but has elements such as figures appropriately stylised.

3,4. These images by Gary Long are pictorially realistic, accurate representations of the characters, yet the 'looser' and more informal rendering provides a distinct evocation of the theme.

7. A typical example of this genre of visual language, Steven Rydberg has given credibility to the physique and three-dimensional placement of the frog, yet the subtlety of distortion and media application suggests an image that is some way from hyperreality.

6

The human figure is also featured extensively on many romantic or historic fiction book jackets. Published biographies also provide opportunities to give character and exaggeration to the features and personality of the subject in question by way of portraiture. There are other forms of illustration that can be classed as stylised realism such as the imagery conceived and produced for young audiences, both non-fiction and narrative fiction. Consider the deliberately contorted figures and elements, either for entertainment purposes or to convey and exaggerate a specific point regarding the individual's character and personality. The fact that these elements are anchored convincingly within the parameters of a pictorial vista suggests a stylised form of realism.

7

'With the exception of iconic or decorative imagery from early times, one of the first movements to deliberately shift from pure realistic representation was impressionism.'

70 Sequential Imagery

What defines sequential imagery? Firstly, it is worth observing that as a visual language, the stylisation of the images can be extremely diverse, but to a degree it is still mainly embedded in pictorial reality, even if some of the elements are wildly distorted and caricatured, they tend to be represented in 'real space', the illusion of a three-dimensional world. The intrinsic nature of sequential imagery is to do with a series of images each following on from the previous to form the essence of the contextual message to be conveyed.

The diversity associated with this type of illustration is not just restricted to elements of style. The sequencing can manifest as moving images: an animated film to be seen as a traditional motion picture, television or forming all or part of an interactive digital package such as within an internet website. It is historically and contemporaneously prevalent as comic books and/or 'picture strips', graphic novels and as narrative fiction and non-fiction material for young audiences.

Contextually, sequential imagery can serve a multitude of purposes: advertising and promotion, information and education, entertainment, packaging and editorial commentary and humour, as seen within the pages of a diverse range of magazines and newspapers.

Historically, sequential imagery was first evidenced during the Palaeolithic period as a series of pictures inscribed on the surfaces of rocks and interior walls of caves. It can be considered the first example of what is understood as 'illustration'. Whilst much is enigmatic to the contemporary eye, some of these prehistoric picture stories can be seen as informing and conveying comment regarding the habitats, environs, status and quality of the game being hunted.

1–3. John Aggs uses the visual language of comic books for this particular sequence yet it is appropriately stylised to be evocative of the theme's historic context.

4,5. Marco Schaaf has produced a sequence appropriated for educational purposes. The visual language of the comic book is considered relevant to both context and given brief.

4

Slightly later, the Egyptians developed hieroglyphics, another form of narrative, visual sequencing combining complex symbolism, pictorial imagery with what is often described as one of the earliest forms of written communication.

Also, another extremely important illustration produced in a historic context must be the Bayeux Tapestry. A continuous sequence of pictorial narratives and descriptions related to the Norman Invasion in 1066, this visual relic is a classic example of early sequential illustration.

These examples exemplify the notion that sequential imagery must be the earliest form of visual language externalised autographically. But how does sequential imagery work and what is its essence?

Most individuals possess an ability to read images in sequence. Nonetheless, it is still important to consider and ensure that the narrative pace and flow of the images correlate both visually and thematically, ensuring comprehension and attention for the prescribed audience. These precepts are particularly important for sequential imagery that is intended for static reproduction on the page or broadsheet.

'Pace' can determine the success or failure of a sequence of images and, as well as being a technical criterion for judgement, this is also an important consideration for ensuring successful receptivity for the reader. The content and unfolding of the narrative, irrespective of its overall length and context, must be of paramount concern when conceiving the visual storyboard. This will determine accents on speed, the length of a continuing or metamorphosing visual syntax, the increase in emphasis regarding drama or detail and when there is a need to cut and proceed immediately to another scenario.

5

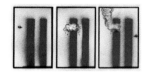

1

72 The attention of the reader or viewer needs to be maintained. It is essential to ensure that the timing regarding the delivery of 'punchlines', the solving of problems and removal of barriers within the narrative is considered with such elements as suspense, drama or surprise.

To conclude, as a visual language the potential for sequential imagery is enormous. The arrival and relentless development of digital technologies will ensure a healthy future for this method of visual communication. It is, however, to be hoped that the aesthetic and highly crafted visual language as exemplified by the traditional animated films and early comic books will continue to bear influence.

2

3

1,4. Peter Kuper's sequential drawings almost assume an animation or even live-action film storyboard identity. An example of cutting edge, editorial comment manifesting as a visual storyline for Fantagraphics Books.

2,3,5. Stephane Gamain conceives a visual sequence with a style that is intelligible and able to convey a pictorial immediacy regarding the unfolding drama. The initial pencil storyboard is included to show first ideas of how the figures might interact.

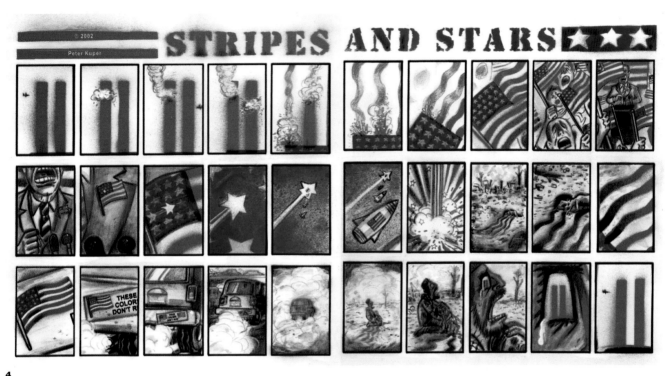

4

5

'Pace can determine the success or failure of a sequence of images and, as well as being a technical criterion for judgement, this is also an important consideration for ensuring successful receptivity for the reader.'

1

2

1,2. A 'mini' sequence by Gary Baseman. Far from pictorial reality it depicts scenic 'real space' in spite of its engagingly animated and surreal concept. The client is 'BLAB!'.

3,4. Thomas Plant informs through this sequence that 'banging your head burns 150 calories an hour'.

3

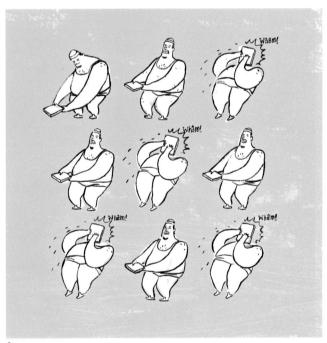

4

'The intrinsic nature
of sequential imagery
is to do with a series
of images each
following on from the
previous to form the
essence of the
contextual message to
be conveyed.'

1

76 **Aesthetics and Non-Aesthetics**

Trends

There has always been, to some extent, trends in illustration, but none so much as with the last three decades. But what is meant by 'trend' in this context? The emphasis here is on visual language and the deliberations assumed regarding the aesthetic or non-aesthetic values placed upon said imagery. However, one cannot overlook the fact that cultural history and association has a considerable influence on the fluctuating facade of contemporary illustration.

This cultural association has facilitated a defined push for some illustration styles to be intrinsically linked with subjects, themes and contexts that are influenced by market culture, most notably the music industry, advertising and fashion.

In recent years, a spate of imagery exemplified by 'ugly' and 'manic' linear drawing has become prevalent within the contexts most associated with certain aspects of market culture.

Urban culture, like punk, new wave and psychedelia before that, has now given rise to a trend in illustration that is symbiotic with the music, fashion and graffiti associated with this. Like many so-called 'subcultures', the influence as spread via the vast extent of the media, is such that society as a whole is touched by it and this type of visual language becomes an accepted norm. As well as traditional contextual uses such as advertising and packaging – most notably music productions and CD covers – the iconic nature of some imagery manifests as a fashion identity, a 'badge' with certain elements printed as designs for T-shirts, bags and other fashion accessories.

Another contemporary trend in illustration visual language is popularly called 'Manga'. Originating from Japan, having permeated the whole of Western society, this is a style of pictorial representation that seemingly does

2

1,3. Alys Jones's fashion illustration entitled 'When in Doubt Wear Red' is economical in rendition, but suitably contemporary in representation.

2. Elizabeth Clements pushes the traditional fashion illustration firmly into contemporary territory with a slightly unnerving figure representation that combines detail with loose and vigorous mark-making.

4,6. Sarah Horne has developed a style of figure representation that is distinctive yet typical of a contemporary trend in illustration: hard-edged and sometimes aggressively distorted images of human stereotypes with a defined urban quality.

5,7. Marina Sagona uses contemporary iconic imagery in these promotional illustrations that are representative of trends in subject matter and visual language.

> 'The emphasis here is on visual language and the deliberations assumed regarding the aesthetic or non-aesthetic values placed upon said imagery.'

3

4

not change in spite of who the exponent might be. Linear, childlike figures characterised by enormous eyes, this is a trend that can either be adored or abhorred!

Whilst one is examining visual language in particular it must be observed that content and subject matter can be considered a benchmark for determining trend.

The fashion industry continues to provide opportunities for illustrators. Historically, imagery that promoted the fashions of the day, most notably from the early 20th century to the 1950s was dominated by illustration. However, the discipline of illustration lost ground to photography and it was not until the 1990s that illustrators have returned to this domain.

Originally, illustrators produced representational drawings and paintings of brands and fashions, images that were used in direct advertising and point of sale. One extremely successful and early exponent of the slick figurative illustration style that influenced much commercial imagery for half a century was the American, Layendecker.

Today, contemporary illustrators engage with either conceptual or literal ideas and will draw from a considerable range of influences, which is dependent on the garments in question and their intended customers. Cult clothing labels will use 'cutting edge' imagery in conjunction with advertising campaigns, which suggests that the illustrations need not be representations of the garments, but an integral component of the thrust and content of the advertising campaign.

Stylistically, it can be considered that some illustrators overlap significantly with surface pattern design such as textiles. If there is too much of an advance into this area then one ceases to produce illustration. Imagery created for point of use and/or for decorative purposes does not normally visually communicate by way of a context.

5

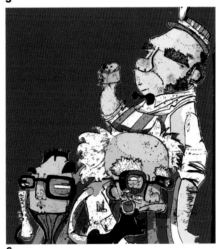

6

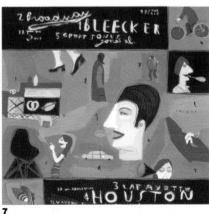

7

78   A considerable distance from fashion there is a certain trend in subject matter which most commonly manifests in portfolios by way of the undergraduate application process, 'Dungeons and Dragons' fantasy. Whilst not considered a trend within the professional commercial parameters of the discipline, such is the popularity of this type of imagery with a certain generation and age group it must be mentioned here.

In a contemporary sense there are numerous and multifarious trends in visual language. Some are associated with media. An example might be a digital illustration which is created by the application of seemingly flat and opaque colour, the overall shape surrounded by a bland and predictably thick, black continuous line.

Other examples suggest the inclusion of hand lettering, intrinsic with the image as a whole, or the representation of specific physical distortions related to the human figure, most notably used in satire. The difference between these examples suggests that it is often difficult to ascertain exactly how to define trends in illustration practice. However, it can be certain that the visual imagery that is illustration is deeply embedded within culture and will continue to represent and communicate either trends in society or be a trend unto itself.

1,2. Dave Kinsey's illustration entitled 'Afro, Harmony, New Era and Token' plays on a distinctly contemporary theme.

3. Fey Dodson's decorative and juxtaposed compositional approach represents a visual language that depicts several aspects that have affirmed trends in illustration, including the enlarged eye and whilst not 'Mangaesque' there has been a trend to distort faces in this manner.

4–6. Jerry LoFaro has taken the theme of 'Chocolate' to new heights of 'Sweet Perfection' with two advertising illustrations.

4

'Chocolate Box'

The term 'chocolate box' is usually associated with imagery that many, particularly some visual arts practitioners would be contemptuous of. It could be said that it is devoid of 'intelligent' aesthetics, superficial, and 'safe' regarding content, particularly as it mainly depicts subject matter that is unchallenging and 'pure', it contextually provides messages that are 'sickly sweet' and overtly sentimental, especially with advertising. These are sweeping generalisations and a more in-depth analysis of what is meant by these clichéd perceptions is required. Much of this type of work pervades the promotional pages of illustrators' agents and representatives' books and websites, suggesting that there is a solid commercial need. But generally, what are the visual characteristics of this style of illustration?

It must be said that even within the curriculum of the most commercially minded and vocational illustration courses, it is a style not usually encouraged. Visually, much of what could be considered 'chocolate box' is a combination of either pictorial or composite hyperreality with distortions of an impressible or sentimentalised nature. The essence of this is more to do with content and subject matter and how it is portrayed.

So, what is it that is depicted and why is it commissioned? In most instances one can associate this as being within the contextual domain of persuasion: advertising, promotions and possibly packaging. A list of product examples might comprise confectionery, pet food, younger children's toys and clothing, travel and vacation destinations. The main aim would be to play on the emotive, desiring, pleasurable, sensual and even hedonistic senses. However, images of 'doleful, wide-eyed children', 'cuddly' kittens and puppies and glistening lashings of cream on 'delicious' hot apple pies are themes that so-called 'intelligent' illustrators would prefer not to undertake if wishing to transcend the level of unadulterated, commercial amorality. Separate the philosophies and ambitions of certain practising or would-be practising illustrators,

5

6

'It contextually provides messages that are "sickly sweet" and overtly sentimental, especially with advertising.'

1

80　isolate the 'chocolate box' imagery and critique objectively. As it has been said before, the most successful illustrations invoke a required reaction or response in one's prescribed audience. Therefore if the product sells, then in some part it must be effective and 'good' illustration. There is another aspect of this type of illustration that has not been mentioned here. Thematically, this is different, more 'adult' in nature and popularly described as 'cheesecake'. Occasionally risqué, the subject matter can be derived from the world of glamour, used to promote or sell a myriad of products, often totally unconnected with the theme and frequently containing elements of humour mixed with sexual connotation. Not to be confused with pornography of any form, this subject matter relies on imagery that is overtly 'chocolate box'; scantily clad and attractive young women, provocatively posed and engaging in some action or commentary that provokes amusement and/or titillation. Whether or not one undertakes to produce imagery of this sort is dependent on personal ethics and adherence or not to aspects of political correctness. Generally, the 'chocolate box' domain of illustration does provide much food for thought and debate regarding levels of aestheticism and individual professional ambition within illustration practice.

'Chocolate Box'

2

1,2. This is an image by Jacques Fabre. Whilst an excellent example of high detail and super-realism, its content and message is overtly sentimentalised in order to advertise the product to its intended and would-be receptive audience.

3,4. Richard Stanley uses 'shock tactics' in this editorial illustration to convey comment regarding accusations made against a certain pop singer.

3

'Shock'

Throughout the ages, artists and more latterly illustrators have produced imagery with the sole intention of inciting disagreeable reactions in the audience. The rationale underpinning such a strategy is usually to present unpalatable truths or suggestions often by way of introducing contentious propositions where there is a requirement. It is sometimes prevalent to observe the sanctity of certain themes and subjects bastardised all in the course of providing deliberate shock.

A list of generalised examples might comprise the following: religion – all faiths lampooned and ridiculed; politics and political leaders – their integrity taken way beyond the edge of acceptable satire to vicious, personal insults; explicit and unnatural sexual practices.

Most of this material can be contextualised as either commentary by way of editorial publications or as narrative fiction, imagery that corresponds with literature of an 'alternative' nature – extreme gothic horror might be an example.

81

4

'Shock'

1

82 What visual language is actually employed? The inherent stylisation can be varied from hyperrealism to extreme forms of surrealism. However, because of the message being conveyed and the nature of the theme or subject, elements within the image or indeed the whole image may be subjected to grotesque and deliberate ugly distortions. These images can be rendered with a raw and irate energy, pushing far beyond the boundaries of traditional and accepted norms regarding composition and pure aesthetics.

This method of working and stylisation has been associated with and embedded within the guise of 'avant-garde' illustration. It can be suggested that whilst some of this imagery may be 'pioneering' and breaking so-called new ground, one has only to recall the 16th-century paintings of the Dutch artist Hieronymus Bosch and his nightmarish and frightening depictions of hell and other demonic themes. 'Shock' imagery has been in existence for a long time.

As a conclusion it might be expedient to deliberate on what relationship aesthetic values manifests with 'chocolate box' and 'shock' illustration. Although presented as extremes in terms of content and contextual thrust, one persuasive and promotional the latter being synonymous with negative comment, satire and narrative, there is a common element recognised in both. It invokes the question of where principles in 'good taste' and the so-called 'appreciation of beauty' may be totally discarded. With 'chocolate box' it might be through ignorance; there are many, some illustrators included, who subscribe to the notion that 'sickly sweet' is to be aesthetic. Alternatively, one can safely assume that a conscious and deliberate discarding of anything aesthetic, however depicted, is the raison d'être underpinning the genre of 'shock' illustration.

2

'Throughout the ages, artists and more latterly illustrators have produced imagery with the sole intention of inciting disagreeable reactions in the audience.'

1,3. Marq Spusta's image for a CD cover appropriately emphasises the title and name of the artiste.

2. Children's narrative fiction? Jaime Zollars creates the antithesis of characterisation and storyline for younger audiences with this illustration from 'Tengu'.

4. David Aronson's distorted and unnerving characterisations present a distinct disregard for 'tasteful' representation by taking this form of person stereotyping to an extreme. A fictional narrative image entitled 'Midway'.

3

4

3

The Role of Illustration

To visually communicate context to audience.

Documentation, Reference and Instruction
An Overview of Illustration for Information
National Curriculum and Trade Material for Young Audiences
Historical and Cultural Subject Matter
Natural Science
Medical Illustration
Technological Subjects
The Illustrator as Scientist and Cultural Historian

Commentary
An Overview of Editorial Illustration
Politics and Current Affairs
'Lifestyle', Reviews and 'Bric-a-Brac'
The Illustrator as Journalist and Commentator

Storytelling
An Overview of Illustration for Narrative Fiction
Picture Books and Early Readers
Comics
The Illustrator as Author of Fiction

Persuasion
Advertising Illustration in Practice
Promotion and the Essence of Advertising

Identity
'Below the Line' and Corporate Branding
Point of Sale and an Overview of Packaging
Books and Music
Illustration and Design

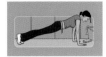

1

86 Documentation, Reference and Instruction

An Overview of Illustration for Information

There has been a popular misconception that illustration produced to convey information must be conventionally realistic and technical both in visual language and in subject matter. It is often thought of as being 'dry' and artistically sterile, devoid of any visual or contextual notions of creativity or innovation. Provided the 'technique' matches the technical details elucidated then its purpose is served. However, it might be important to consider that the domain of illustration practice that documents, provides reference, education, explanation and instruction is contextually very broad and covers a myriad of themes and subjects. Also, the complete visual language associated with information illustration can be considerably diverse: literal, pictorial representations, simple or complex sequential imagery, conceptual and diagrammatic solutions. Methods and processes of mark-making and use of media can be equally multifarious from state of the art digital rendering to every possible application contained within the parameters of autography. As a conclusion, the assumption that hyperrealism under the guise of 'technical illustration' is the dominant visual language, then it must be pronounced that where appropriate – audience and thematic considerations permitting – decorative, impressionistic and painterly approaches are frequently utilised.

2

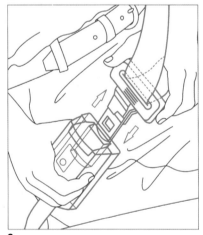

3

3. Pure information illustration is succinct, unambiguous and pragmatic: Ben Hasler has produced an image that demonstrates an 'exceedingly functional seatbelt'.

2. Hyperrealism is synonymous with reference illustration. This is no exception as Martin Macrae provides ultimate detail to a modern timepiece.

4,6. From as far back as Classical times, maps are one of the earliest forms of drawn images to provide information: Jo Goodberry has conceived an illustrated version of East Anglia demonstrating the best in contemporary map design.

1,5. Ruth Thomlevold uses a stylised and economic use of line and colour yet the information is clear, unambiguous and undisguised. These images are entitled 'Kitchen Gym Exercises' for a non-fiction publication.

4

Historically, when did the need arise to provide information by visual means? From the early 19th century, a person was not considered fully educated unless they had a broad, deep and detailed knowledge of all areas of culture and human endeavour. This was expected to include a solid grounding in the scientific disciplines, an appreciation of art in all its manifestations, a store of mythological references and tales, considerable knowledge of geological wonders and oddities, plus curiosity about technological developments that were changing the face of society at the time. The Industrial Revolution gave way for the original engineering feats of Isambard Kingdom Brunel; the march of exploration and discovery facilitated the likes of Charles Darwin to revolutionise concepts of nature and evolution.

The physical and intellectual world of the 19th century started to be captured and categorised by way of innumerable complex and painstakingly precise illustrations, evidenced at the time by black-and-white line and tonal engravings. These images were to be found in volumes that in some way mirror the array of non-fiction publications produced today: educational textbooks of a rudimentary nature and for the advanced level students; popular reference books and encyclopaedias. Practically every subject known to humankind was subjected to immense visual scrutiny and research by the Victorian Age illustrators and engravers – mathematics and astronomy; physics and meteorology; chemistry, mineralogy and geology; botany; zoology; anthropology, human anatomy and surgery; geography and planography; history and ethnology; military sciences; architecture; mythology and religious rites; the fine arts; technology.

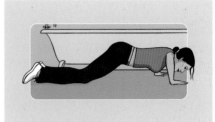

5

6

'The domain of illustration practice that documents, provides reference, education, explanation and instruction is contextually very broad and covers a myriad of themes and subjects.'

88 The nature of this imagery, its precision, delicacy and attention to detail, the authoritativeness of the treatment provided the 'yardstick' and influence by which this context of illustration practice evolved. Time progressed with the emergence of 20th-century technical illustration. Predominantly black and white and exceedingly functional, usually for a narrowly prescribed audience requiring instruction from technical manuals, the content was often 'lost' on the 'uninitiated' viewer. However, this domain of visual communication progressed via the airbrush 'craze' of the 1970s and 1980s into rich, full-colour renditions of a vast multitude of themes and subjects, aimed at an immense worldwide audience. New media outlets such as the internet and global television, its programmes and websites enhanced by state-of-the-art digital static and moving imagery, has provided the 21st century 'technical illustrator' with a much more intoxicating and creative rationale and challenge. The complex, richly colourful encyclopaedias and popular reference books that first appeared during the 1960s and early 1970s, set precedents and standards related to hyperreal imagery, composite and imaginative diagrams and representations. The Mitchell Beazley published set of encyclopaedias entitled collectively 'The Joy of Knowledge' could be described as the catalyst for much material of this nature. These publications allowed the domain of natural science illustration to achieve new heights of status and authority.

'Generally speaking, illustration is a great instructional medium. Information can be ingested more readily when conveyed visually.'

1,4. Hannah McVicar's botanical illustrations give clear identification regarding species yet are distinctly evocative of the early decorative approaches to image creation.

2,3. Information illustration can take many forms provided the message is unambiguous. Here Marjorie Dumortier uses humour and comic distortion to visually describe ballet terms.

5. A classic example of early technical illustration, an engraving that elucidates detail of a railway locomotive from a bygone age.

Enchainment

Pas de danse

Sur les pointes

Cambré

2

3

So what is the status and circumstance of this context of illustration practice today?

Generally speaking, illustration is a great instructional medium. Information can be ingested more readily when conveyed visually. An engagement with learning and research or the acquisition of reference material, whether in an educational, professional or recreational context, can be considered a more palatable and enjoyable experience if one is acquiring knowledge by ways that either entertain, provide interaction, or amuse. In order for this to occur, the source of information must transcend the role of basic provider. This, in a large part, can be facilitated by the creative and innovative use of illustration.

Information illustration works on many levels. It can elucidate the practicalities of physical construction or performance; the manufacture and erection of engineering or architectural structures; the playing of musical instruments, sports or games. It can also provide guidance, thought and explanation of simple or complex processes.

4

5

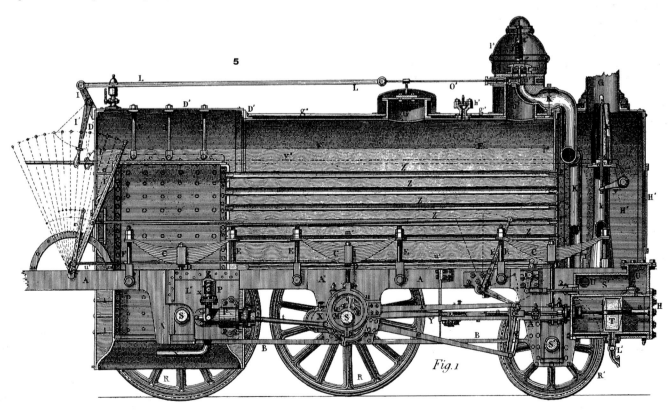

Fig. 1

90

Examples might comprise the following which are either associated with the natural world or intellectual in concept: historical and political dynasties; ecosystems and food chains; taxonomies such as animal and plant classifications; biological functions such as respiration, reproduction and digestion; the theory of evolution; crop cultivation and food processing.

It is interesting to note that many associated with both the creative industries and education will connect the visual language of sequential imagery solely with the context of fictional storytelling. The aforementioned examples are fundamentally embedded in a sequence of events and can thus manifest as 'story'. Narrative and sequential imagery are appropriate visual languages to employ when conceiving ideas to communicate information. Is not the 'Life and Career of Julius Caesar' a story? The metamorphosis of an insect? Or the first manned journey to the moon!?

The following list provides an insight into the many and varied media and publishing outlets associated with information illustration: non-fiction gift books, CDs and encyclopaedias; specialist technical reference publications; children's non-fiction books both trade and retail, and educational; television documentaries; magazines; company reports and other corporate material; the worldwide web; interactive, educational games.

To conclude, illustration is the only discipline within the realm of the visual arts and communications that explains or elucidates information. Much of what is seen by way of this contextual domain is the creation and interpretation of new knowledge. It must therefore be right that illustrators are afforded much respect and authority regarding the subjects they visualise. The insatiable need within society to gain knowledge, the progress of science, technology and culture will ensure that this aspect of illustration practice will not only consolidate, but increase in its importance as a context of visual communication.

1,2. Kirsty Thomson uses a decorative yet highly evocative visual language to present a concept entitled 'Honey Facts'.

'Illustration is the only discipline
within the realm of the visual arts and
communications that explains or
elucidates information. Much of what
is seen by way of this contextual
domain is the creation and
interpretation of new knowledge.'

1

92   National Curriculum and Trade Material for Young Audiences

Non-fiction books for children represent one of the biggest operations in publishing, particularly in terms of the number of books sold and read. This can be attributed to the fact that there are two principal sales outlets: trade or retail and national or state curriculum.

Trade books, sold in bookshops, ordered online or purchased by way of mail order include the majority of popular non-fiction subjects; natural history, science and technology, prehistoric life, sport, astronomy and space travel, history, geography and computer science. There are also numerous themes and concepts for early learners, such as counting books, alphabets and dictionaries. National curriculum titles are directly associated with school or college syllabi and replicate many of the aforementioned subjects. They also include the more academically challenging course-work literature associated with assessment and examination.

Although these two aspects of non-fiction publishing for children replicate much in terms of content and subjects there is a distinct division and it is to do with audience perception in relation to what the books are for. Trade books, purchased either by the intended audience, their parents or guardian provide the reader with information and knowledge that they generally seek whereby there is already an inherent interest in the subject. National curriculum titles are perceptively imposed upon the reader. However, an examination of the shelves in many school libraries will reveal a dramatic crossover. Many books are published and sold through both channels.

This context of illustration practice, visualising and presenting facts to a young audience, is an extensive and important area and requires a multitude of applications and considerations. The illustrator must be able to empathise and engage with the subject and explore, where necessary, all avenues of research. It is often expected, either by previous experience, by prior knowledge and learning or by specialist qualification that the illustrator adopt a position of authority having expertise and insight regarding content.

2

3

Nile Crocodile
in the
Luangua River Valley

by Schuyler Bull
illustrated by Alan Male

4

5

ALONG
the LUANGWA

A Story of an
African Floodplain

by Schuyler Bull
Illustrated by
Alan Male

1–5. A case study by the author: a book for four- to eight-year olds. It is usual for the illustrator to design the cover, and conceive all visual aspects of the book's interior. A pencil visual of the cover is required for approval prior to artwork completion. The thumbnail sketch of the first double-page spread will reveal the need for a slight change when producing the final illustration; the crocodile appeared too scary for the young audience so its mouth has been suitably closed up!

6–8. Natural science features extensively within the remit of non-fiction material for young audiences. The author has illustrated these complete books and designed the covers.

6

There is often joint authorship when commissioned by the publisher with collaboration between a writer and illustrator. This means that one has a certain amount of responsibility regarding the choice of subject matter and the content of the book. Also, the illustrator will be expected to contribute to the overall design concept: design, layout and cover. One must also have a working knowledge and understanding of the narrative and sequential pacing and flow of the book.

The need to educate and impart knowledge to an age group that is born into an already stimulating, multimedia world means there has never been such a need to bring learning to life. Innovation and creativity becomes an important aspect of the conceptual and practical process. 'Stuffy' uninteresting images such as 'dead looking' animals, cut to white on the page and without visual interaction will not do any more.

Many books allude to notions of narrative and entertainment by imparting information via 'fun' characters or locations, introduced over and above the fundamental subject matter, but symbiotic with the main theme. An example might be an anthropomorphous animal taking the reader through a sequence of 'stop-off' destinations on a journey of discovery. Interactive and engaging features such as 'pop-ups', transparent pages and other devices are synonymous with much published material of this nature. Many comprise or are part of other media packages, such as CD encyclopaedias or games.

The variety and diversity of subject matter covered will often require different approaches regarding concept and visual language. An example will be natural history. Concern for the natural world is firmly embedded in everyday life from the classroom to television news bulletins: the conservation and protection of the environment; rainforests; depleted habitats of fauna close to extinction; the pollution of air, land and sea; global warming. These are topics that constantly inspire the publication of books for the very young, junior school leavers and beyond.

7

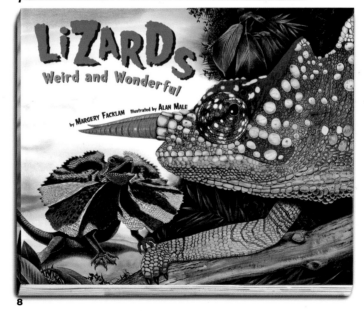

8

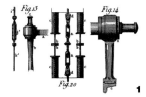

1

94 But there are some general principles. For example, most books about animals in particular should conform to one of the two methods given for presenting the subject matter. The first is taxonomic. This is where classifications or specific family groupings establish the format of the table of contents. Examples might be 'Birds of Prey', 'Dragonflies' or 'Whales and Dolphins'.

The second is largely based on depicting the inhabitants of a particular environment, biome, ecosystem or habitat. A selection of themes could include the following: the coral reef, the ecology of an oak tree, the South American rainforests, North European lakes and rivers. There are principles associated with other subjects. Publications that present practical 'how it works' material should also consider entertaining and engaging approaches to the manner in which the information is imparted. Often, the subject matter is extremely 'technical' in its inherent nature: complex contemporary architectural vistas, exploded views of historic buildings, ships, aircraft or railway locomotives. Where appropriate, the economic, sensitively applied and under-indulgent use of line and mark-making will, when connected with an innovative use of colour and holding graphic devices such as leader lines, give clarity and information with an aesthetic ambience.

The visual inclusion of associated material with a topic or theme can also give a value-added dimension to the overall image.

An example might be a highly detailed and accurate reconstruction of Stephenson's 1829 steam railway locomotive 'Rocket', cut to white on the page, its immediate and surrounding environment conspicuous by its absence. This image would undoubtedly be brought to life with the locomotive depicted in situation with men on horseback in pursuit, small children running beside the track giving chase, aristocratic women holding kerchiefs to their faces in grimace at the grime and smell! It is not only important to introduce narrative and drama, but also the context of a subject is an essential educative precept to consider for one's prescribed audience. Perception of a subject's visual appearance can be considered as

2

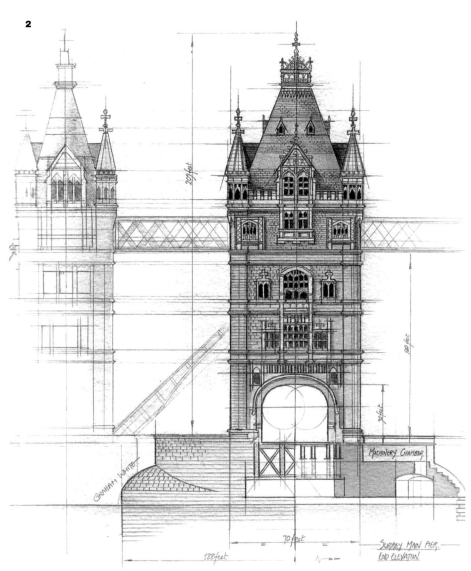

1. Engravings from the early Victorian era that give detail to mechanical function.

2,3. Architecture combined with history: Graham White's illustrations have a traditional autographic quality.

4. This pictorial representation of the Titanic by David Young is an example of a style of illustration well suited to provide a narrative historic flavour and documentation for its young audience.

3

96 having 'surface' knowledge. But understanding the subject's inherent rationale for existence such as how, why, when and with what is to possess far deeper and meaningful insights and comprehension.

Picture books for early readers form a large and important aspect of young audience non-fiction material. Exciting and colourful illustration can facilitate a child's initial familiarity with words and letterforms. The introduction of problem solving such as an invitation to locate a hidden character or element within a complex and entertaining scenario can provide interaction with the essence of what is being taught. Hidden clues and messages related to numbers, shapes, letters and simple words are all aspects exemplified by the clichéd, but veracious statement 'to make learning fun'.

The nature of imagery used in informational books for children can be exceptionally diverse, dependent on the overall design concept and subject matter. However, one must not lose sight of the need for objectivity and where relevant the accurate representation of subject matter. It is also perilous to neglect the needs of the prescribed audience.

There should be an avoidance of superficiality and reliance purely related to fashion regarding the style of illustrations.

'Picture books for early readers form a large and important aspect of young audience non-fiction material.'

1

3

Dit is de schatkamer. Hier zie je onder een afdak een verguilde houten kist staan. De godin Isis bewaakt een albasten binnenkist met vier vakken. In deze vakken liggen vier heel kleine doodskisten met Toetanchamons longen, lever, darmen en maag.

2

OP ZOEK NAAR TOETANCHAMON

SUE CLARKE   LEMNISCAAT

The contextual thrust must be evident; do the images convey information accurately, lucidly and appropriately regarding one's given audience? Do the illustrations educate with some notion of entertainment and do they relate to and complement the text? Is there or does there need to be an element of narrative and does the pace and flow of the sequencing of imagery work throughout the book?

It is important that one's own visual language regarding the illustration should not be compromised and that one's work is afforded respect and produced with integrity.

1–4. Educative and general information books for young audiences often contain illustrations that are engaging and evocative of the subject matter, but also work as entertaining, innovative and interactive concepts. This book entitled 'Tombs of the Pharaohs' designed and illustrated by Sue Clarke is no exception.

1

98 ■ **Historical and Cultural Subject Matter**

There has always been a need to visually reconstruct themes and subjects associated with human history. The ability to give resurrection and life to the past through the discipline of illustration will forever be in demand. Even when there is photographic evidence of the period, illustration can go much further and recreate events with much more detail and exposition.

The work of the historical and cultural illustrator can be evidenced and encountered by way of a variety of forms and media outlets: children's information and reference books; encyclopaedias; specialist historical, anthropological or archaeological publications and research papers; television documentaries; films and motion pictures; magazines and newspapers; museums and other learned institutions.

The rationale and origination of the work can be equally as diverse; sometimes seen in the popular media sensationalising a fresh theory or evidence as substantiated by newly uncovered documentation or archaeological finds to being endemic with systematic, erudite and ordered research. The subject matter is vast and provides opportunities for illustrators of various persuasions and backgrounds. Again the breadth of working practice and visual language can be immense. One example might be where the illustrator is employed providing black-and-white line and tone drawings of artefacts and topography for an archaeological field unit. Another example might suggest research for 'high end' television programmes and films.

1. An early Victorian 'cutaway' illustration depicting the interior of a galleon.

2. Oliver Hurst's reconstruction of the Battle of Trafalgar is afforded a traditional visual treatment. It does, however, have a certain academic value related to its content: this scene from the battle has never been visualised before and the placement and identification of vessels has been appropriated by original research.

2

1

100 This domain of practice provides opportunities for illustrators who have professional or specialist qualifications, experience or lay insights into the subject matter. Those whose general abilities lie with the pictorial representation of the human form may also find employment within this category.

The most specialist field of historical and cultural illustration is firmly established and embedded within the disciplines of anthropology and archaeology. Here, the illustrator plays an important part in the accurate and controlled collection of data, painstakingly documented in the field and put into published form. Anthropology is the study of cultures; archaeology that of human antiquities. Both are intrinsically linked.

The essence of this work is collaboration between experts and the illustrator; a direct interface between the subject discipline and visual arts practice. The principal aim is research and the presentation of new knowledge. This suggests that the illustrator must adhere to standard conventions of working practice when producing the completed drawings. The academic and professional community will expect no other and there is no room to allow artistic license to even slightly 'run amok'. The subject matter should be visually reconstructed lucidly and economically and one should employ a standard ink line and stipple technique whether rendered digitally or autographically. An example of a page layout for an archaeological research document might formulate thus: the concise arrangement of artefactual material such as Palaeolithic stone tools and weapons into functional or stylistic assemblages; light source (if any) indicated from the left; the inclusion of scale; projectiles arranged with points up; stone implements with striking edges shown pointed down.

An illustrator who adheres rigidly to these strictures should, in essence have an overriding empathy and desire to engage deeply with the subject matter.

In previous times, artists were often commissioned to produce large-scale paintings of glorious military endeavours and

2

3

1,3. Historical illustration in context: an engraving that depicts an 18th-century French galleon produced approximately 100 years after the scene being depicted and now regarded as a classic example of Victorian information illustration.

2. Battles provide much visual drama and a contextual reason to convey violent, yet historically meaningful descriptions of the horror of warfare. Reconstructions of this nature require much attention to detail and accuracy regarding clothing, weapons and the placement and interaction of figures. This illustration by Eivind Bøvor is a battle from Viking history.

4. Alberto Guerra depicts a popular topic, particularly within the pages of children's history books; a Roman battle scene.

5. It is often necessary to produce historic visual reconstructions that depict the reality of daily life without the usual ingredient of high drama and action. Phil Kenning provides a glimpse at medieval 'Spon Street'.

'The essence of this work is collaboration between experts and the illustrator; a direct interface between the subject discipline and visual arts practice.'

4

victories, depictions of human subjugation – a defeated foe or political enemy, the signings of treaties and surrenders, the exploits of exploration and discovery. Often at the behest of state or aristocratic patronage, the essence was propagandist, ensuring the 'right' information was being conveyed.

In a contemporary context, it is common to observe and encounter such work. However, there is a distinct difference, that being it is produced for documentary, information or educative purposes. The rationale is objectivity and where possible the accurate representation of content and subject matter. Themes such as 'subjugation', slavery and the patronisation of so-called 'primitive cultures' have ceded to respect and understanding. The dioramas and actual size three-dimensional reconstructions of Native American history and culture as seen at the New York State Museum are testament to this.

Battle scenes are recreated depicting the same amount of 'violence' and inherent vehemence embedded within the nature of the subject, but at the same time based on credible and accountable research. Observe the strict editorial control subjected to the content of such work commissioned for the National Geographic Magazine.

Children's books and other associated media such as CDs provide a rich and varied gathering of cultural and historical subjects to be illustrated and described. Pictorial and where appropriate decorative reconstructions of all aspects of human history from the time of the earliest peoples to notions of the future! There is today, unlike the jingoistic thrust of equivalent publications up until the 1950s, an emphasis placed on the depiction of everyday life, the inclusion of aspects and themes related to all layers of society. Typical examples might include the following: domestic life, transport, social and cultural interaction, politics, conflict and religion.

The digital age has provided opportunities to recreate the past (and the future) by way of life-like, animated hyperreality. The advent of this medium has meant that television documentary-makers and the motion picture

5

'The inherent skills associated with representational illustration practice: good draughtsmanship and human figure drawing; the ability to visualise and display by way of drawing complex scenes of human interaction; the use of composition, space and light.'

1

102 industry can present material that is
unblemished and unhindered by the distraction
of substandard special effects. Theoretically, the
audience can now become totally immersed
with content.

So where does the illustrator contribute to
this genre of image-making? The popularity
of archaeology programmes such as Channel
Four's 'Time Team', BBC Television
documentaries such as 'Horizon' and the
many and varied productions seen on the
Discovery and History channels often
demand complex visual reconstructions
embedded in reality. The return in popularity
of historical 'epics' to the cinema screen has
in recent years required much visual research
and attention to detail. Despite the emphasis
on entertainment some elements are still
couched in factual realism. Working within
this domain, illustrators research, storyboard,
draw characters and costumes as a prequel to
progression with filming and production.
This is an essential contribution facilitated by
insight and empathy with the subject and all
of the inherent skills associated with
representational illustration practice: good
draughtsmanship and human figure drawing;
the ability to visualise and display by way of
drawing complex scenes of human
interaction; the use of composition, space
and light.

To conclude, historical and cultural
illustration provides a considerable and
valuable understanding of the breadth of
richness of this subject matter whatever
medium and output it is expressed through.

1–3. The lives of
individuals from past
societies provide
interesting historic
insights. Phil Kenning
documents the artisan
world of the fletcher and
medieval blacksmith.

2

1

104 Natural Science

Scientific and technical illustration is a domain of practice that in terms of subject matter is vast and expansive. It is also a discipline that first came in to existence in Classical times when scribes and illuminators observed and recorded details of the natural world, including aspects of human anatomy. As has been mentioned before, the Renaissance period gave rise to an intense and prolific interaction between science and art with protagonists claiming association with both vocations. This brought about the claim that science and art can be one and the same, a view held today substantiated by the nature of working practice as exemplified by many so-called 'scientist-illustrators'. The subsequent drawings from the Renaissance, many by the likes of Leonardo da Vinci, have become synonymous with early scientific and technological research, many of these images firmly established as an important genre of study related to art and science history. Throughout latter periods it would appear that the subject matter was always the 'driving force' regarding the development and professional success of the artist/illustrators. Knowledge and understanding of anatomy, the natural world, architecture and technology, underpinned the imagery produced and in many cases was the reason for its production.

The British artist Stubbs, known for his detailed portraits of horses, was so well versed in the anatomy of his subjects he was considered to be almost as knowledgeable as a veterinary surgeon. The American Audubon, one of the earliest and most successful illustrators of bird life set new precedents in standards, not only in artistic quality but provided one of the first essential visual guides for avian recognition. The Italian Canaletto brought the craft of architectural illustration to new heights of detail with his evocative Venetian vistas. Finally, a volume that is still in print and available in bookshops, 'The Concise British Flora in Colour' by the late Reverend Keble Martin is considered to be the ultimate reference for this subject matter. Produced throughout the 20th century it represents a life's work of total engagement with this topic, expressed through illustration that is

2

1,2,4. John James Audubon, an American naturalist, produced these striking illustrations as part of a collection entitled 'Birds of North America' in 1827. Widely regarded as the father of full-colour natural history illustration, his attention to detail, lifelike poses and characterisations set precedents that devalued the work of his contemporaries whose imagery bore too much resemblance to their taxidermic reference material.

3,5. Many 18th- and 19th-century engravings of natural science subject matter were embarrassingly inaccurate representations by today's standards. However, these botanical illustrations convey strict adherence to detail.

3

renowned for its meticulous attention to detail. These examples, whilst embedded within the visual arts, are representative of an overwhelming fellowship and connection with the topic, the subject matter being all important. This concept is predominant within the domain of practice today. Without the need to bind and interlock with the subject, there would be no illustration of this kind.

So, what is scientific illustration? It can be described as 'art at the service of science'. It is the production of literal, representational images of measured accuracy and other graphic devices such as diagrams that communicate all aspects related to the field of science. In a contemporary context it can be found in the equivalent form and media outlets as its historical and cultural illustration counterpart from dedicated research publications to popular media exposure.

In a pure sense, scientific illustration communicates subtleties and eliminates the ambiguities of language. It is this that makes it an important and often necessary element in precise communication.

Within the culture and practice of scientific research, the illustrator whose training, ability and interests extend both into art and science, applies discipline to creativity so that the images produced do not merely decorate, but serve science. The successful scientific illustrator must have a penchant for precision, great tolerance for and appreciation of detailed work.

Exemplars of good practice particularly when related to scientific collaboration and new knowledge-based research might show where the imagery may depict diagnostic characters that may differentiate one taxonomic group from another, it may clarify infinite focal depth and overlapping layers, emphasise important details and reconstruct incomplete physical evidences, results unattainable through photographic means.

4

5

1

106

A prerequisite for unadulterated scientific illustration practice would be a dedication to turning natural truths into pictorial truths, a taste for the facts and facets of natural history and its associated subjects and for biological and cultural research.

A breakdown and examination of the subjects appointed to within the parameters of scientific illustration will reveal an extraordinary broad and intense reservoir of knowledge.

The immediate factor is that the overall domain of natural science is divided into two distinct divisions; the life sciences and the earth sciences. The life sciences include what is generally described as natural history: the taxonomies and ecologies of zoology and botany; and biology, the systems and processes of life's functions including anatomy. The earth sciences are represented by geology, oceanography, meteorology, astronomy and vulcanology.

There is also another classification of scientific study that enjoys a unique overlap with both major domains; palaeontology. A blend of geology and natural history it is basically the study of life in the prehistoric past. It is worth examining the effectiveness of illustration as a means to visually convey prehistoric life forms factually, particularly for a wide audience. A review of the debates surrounding this subject certainly until the 1980s, shows that most people saw dinosaurs in particular as artists have depicted them from the mid-19th century sketches based on scanty fossil evidence. The American illustrator Charles Knight was a protagonist regarding the first representations of prehistoric life and his work set a standard which was followed everywhere. His masterpiece is a set of murals in Chicago's Field Museum of Natural History.

2

3

4

However, recent scientific analysis of prehistoric animal behaviour and physical mechanics, have inspired new ways of visual representation. Instead of sluggish reptilian attitudes we now see the creatures as rearing, sprinting and 'lively'. Images of this nature are ubiquitous. The popularity of books on this subject, and the extent and quality of the displays in museums around the world, has never been so great or considerable.

But it is the digital animations and animatronics as seen on television or in the cinema that have ascended new heights regarding standards of representation and dramatic effect. This overtly 'hyperreal' visual concept should combine with scientific fact and theory to determine an approach and stylisation required of illustrators ensuring that reconstructions are authoritative, dynamic and lifelike.

An appealing subject matter for illustrators and audiences of all descriptions is the study of animal life. There are numerous volumes and publications associated with this from small, inexpensive 'pocket guides' to large formal 'quality' editions all lavishly illustrated in full-colour providing both reference and identification and representation in habitat or ecosystem. Birdlife of all descriptions, mammals such as big cats and other popular inhabitants of zoological gardens, butterflies and other insects, freshwater, marine and aquarium fish are just a selection of the many themes and topics covered.

5

6

2. Martin Macrae induces an almost photographic quality to the vista of this marine environment: ecosystems and organic interaction are important subjects to be visually recreated by the illustrator.

Dinosaurs are one of the most popular subjects regarding non-fiction material for books and TV documentaries. They also feature as a fictional supporting cast in both historic and contemporary motion pictures. All of this provides much work for the illustrator who has to be abreast of current paleontological research and thinking regarding appearance and visual attitudes. Martin Macrae **3.** and the author **1,5,6,7.** provide scenic, interactive reconstructions and individual details to certain species.

4. A typical example of an image produced for species identification: a straightforward pose, cut to white. The author depicts a common European frog.

7

1

108 The use of illustration in this context often competes with photography. However, its use can be clearly justified. In addition to the standard portrayal of the animal's physical form, the illustrator can convey a sense of vitality and essence of the animal, much as might be experienced in the field. In contrast, photography only captures a fleeting moment in an animal's life. Natural history illustration is often used in publications to balance the spontaneity of photography with a more reflective view of the subject, or to depict behaviours and situations not easily photographed. An image of this nature should be a summation of the illustrator's informed impressions of the animal's typical attitudes, habitat and anatomy. The illustrator has the freedom to transcend the vagaries and arbitrariness of an individual animal in a particular situation, to bring to the audience a more profound insight into the ecology of a species.

The type of illustration thus described must not be confused with what is popularly known as 'wildlife art'. This genre of populist imagery cannot be classed as illustration as it normally rests beyond the boundaries of any recognisable context. As a visual language it is more often than not 'chocolate box' in style. In reproduced form it would be more frequently encountered on greetings cards in retail outlets that might also specialise in the sale of mass-produced framed prints.

To conclude, the remit of natural science illustration demands an approach that ensures the imagery in question is as true as possible to its subject upon publication or broadcast and will supplement a body of scientific information with authority and integrity.

3

1. The author provides a detailed close-up of the 'website' of a crab spider.

2,3. The author presents two invertebrate subjects in traditional 'set' pose cut to white and visually arranged for ease of identification; a treatment and visual language ideal to provide a hyper-detailed physical exposé of very small organisms.

'Natural science illustration
demands an approach that
ensures the imagery in question
is as true as possible to its
subject.'

1

110 Medical Illustration

The vocation of medical illustration can be traced as far back as the Middle Ages. However, these early exponents did not make reference to dissected cadavers or other appropriate 'hands on' evidence. The Italian anatomist Vesalius can be considered the true father of medical illustration, his woodblock produced in Titian's studio circa 1543 and entitled 'De Humani Corporis Fabrica' displays an obvious indication of direct observation. The start of this procedure, the binding of original research with effective technique, brought medical practice out of the age of superstition and mistaken adherence to unproven theory. Contemporary medical illustration practice is demanding and diverse. It is an extremely specialised field. To engage professionally one must be fully conversant in medical terminology, human anatomy, the available reference materials and the proper procedures for working in a medical and surgical environment. It is often essential to undertake specialist undergraduate or postgraduate study and it is this training for working closely with other medical professionals that most distinguishes the medical illustrator from other scientific illustration disciplines.

The core aspect of the medical illustration vocation is to produce anatomical and surgical illustrations for education and training purposes. It can be said that effective medical illustration can be as life enhancing as a good medical procedure. Doctors, physicians and nursing professionals learn much from the anatomical renderings embedded in their texts. This work can also involve the production of three-dimensional illustrations – medical sculptures also used to augment anatomical training. In this context the medical illustrator may conduct a practice within a large academic research or teaching institution. Some may have faculty or staff positions in schools of medicine or allied health professions providing visual material for research publications and medical and surgical texts written by the faculty members.

The work produced must be approached pragmatically with ultimate attention to detail. The visual language should be lucid

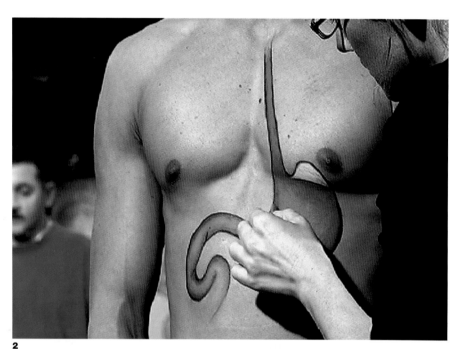

2

3

1–3. Juliet Percival produced illustrations that identified the location of internal organs when painted directly on to the naked bodies of living humans, for a Channel Four programme entitled 'Live Anatomy'.

4,5. Visual aesthetics and a concern for 'good taste' prevails as an important criterion regarding contemporary medical illustration. Juliet Percival's superimposed representations of inflammatory arthritis and the economic, yet informative visual simplicity of the accompanying vignette are excellent examples.

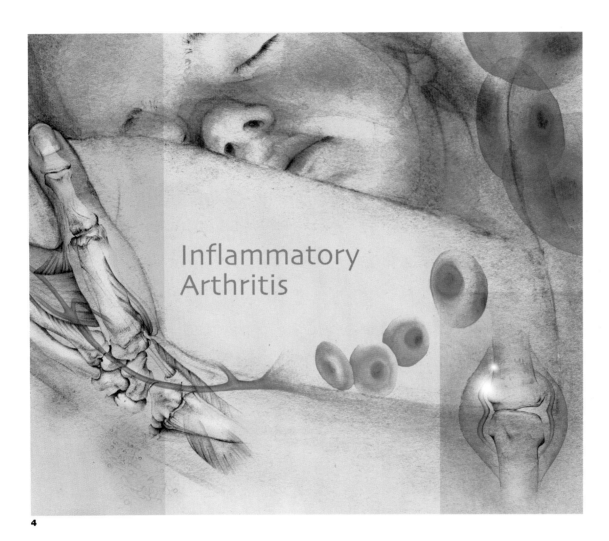

Inflammatory
Arthritis

4

5

'Contemporary medical
illustration practice is
demanding and diverse. It is
an extremely specialised field.
To engage professionally one
must be fully conversant in
human anatomy.'

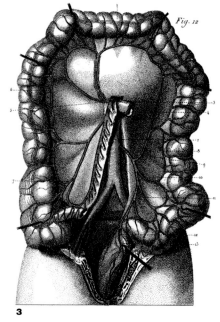

Fig. 16 **1**

112 yet succinct, facilitating an immediate engagement with the subject matter. These working processes can present certain problems. One is dealing with human subject matter which may bestow practical or ethical difficulties thus complicating aspects of research for visual reference material. Because of necessity one may be obliged to work from a reference source that is much less direct than those engaged by other illustrators. Frequently, the condition or procedure to be illustrated must be reconstructed from consultations with the appropriate medical practitioner, or from photographic depictions of actual patients or surgery.

Another aspect of medical illustration defines a status considered to be more commercial in practice and more contemporary regarding its media placement and visual language. This is a domain that is removed from the field of education and training and placed firmly within the realm of trade publishing and popular media such as television. Themes and subjects will comprise anatomical and human biological processes to the presentation of new theories and discoveries. This work can be seen on the pages of 'quality' encyclopaedias and reference books, pharmaceutical company promotional and informative literature, on the covers of or featuring predominantly within popular magazines such as 'Scientific American' or 'New Scientist' and providing much elucidation to the contents and themes of television documentary programmes.

Whilst the accent is on the provision of accurate information, the visual language can be a much more 'sumptuous' form of stylisation as opposed to the 'frugality' of pure educative material. Rich and colourful, highly detailed literal and conceptual images rendered to the highest standards of autographic or digital finish: a 'space age' image with a 'galaxy' of cells floating in a sea of bodily fluid; an athlete in full flow with a visual superimposition of healthy straining muscles seen through transparent skin; a sequence of images depicting the treatment, healing process and full recovery of a serious injury – the 'patient' being both generic and 'attractive'. Much emphasis is placed on

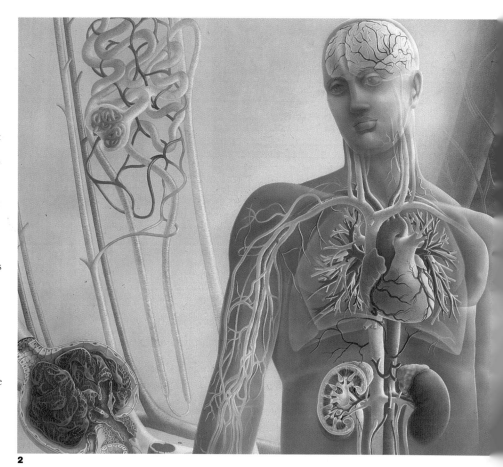

2

1,3. The Victorian Age saw great advancements in medical practice, facilitated by a deeper understanding of anatomy and biological function. This is an engraving that shows the vascular system.

2. Jean-Claude Michel produces intensely detailed and conceptually rich medical landscapes. This illustration (rendered traditionally in oil on canvas) makes reference to cardio vascular and renal operation and function.

4. Anita Kunz utilises the art of medical illustration for an editorial context: the cover of 'The New York Times Magazine'.

5. Juliet Percival provides simplicity and aesthetic sensitivity to this pregnancy sequence.

Fig. 12

3

ensuring an adherence to 'good taste' regarding the presentation of subject matter and aesthetics with visual language. The human subjects and models are represented as healthy and fit; it is no longer acceptable to depict cadavers with exposed internal organs removed for exposition amid shreds of peeled back skin and flayed muscle! The days of glorifying a bloody autopsy by painting or illustration is now something of the past. Such is the importance regarding research, education, the thirst for new knowledge and the expeditious progress of discovery – the demand for high quality medical illustration will undoubtedly intensify.

4

5

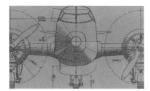

1

114 Technological Subjects

Technical illustration is principally a visual exposition of manufactured and constructed matter. Its chief concern is to elucidate structure, function and mechanics.

The technical illustrator must adhere to criteria that is fundamental to the success of the work; the balance of detail and information with legibility and usefulness and the converting of what is often basic reference material into a correctly projected drawing. The subject matter is always three-dimensional, but the requirement is more often than not for reproduction in a flat two-dimensional style or animated digitally expressing volumatic representation through a screen-based medium. It is important for one to have insight and understanding of the principles of engineering and a familiarity and tangency with some of the subject matter most frequently illustrated. Furthermore one must engage with a practical employment of geometry and three-dimensional drawn construction along with all aspects of perspective from basic applications to the most advanced. The skills employed must not be assumed as being 'dry' with all draughtsmanship and detail; in the hands of the best practitioners, contemporary technical illustration is both evocative and exciting.

2

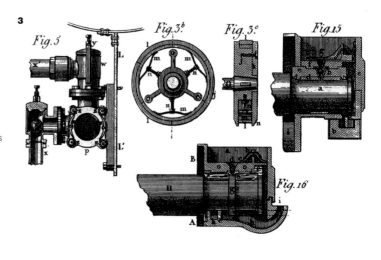

3

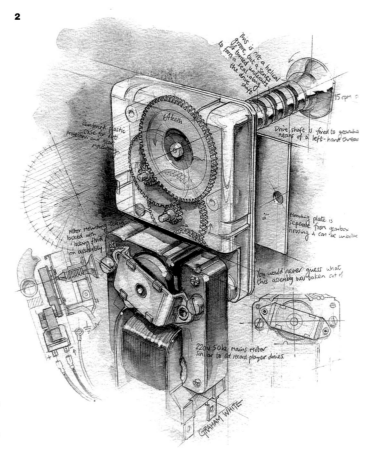

1. Graham White's drawing of the front view of an aeroplane shows perfect visual symmetry and attention to detail.

2. A traditional rendition of a complex mechanism by Graham White that is both informative and detailed, yet the seemingly 'free drawn' technical construction provides an added aesthetic.

3,4. Technical drawings facilitated the design and construction of engineering and architectural projects as far back as classical times. The industrial revolution initiated a sudden increase in this type of imagery with

information and knowledge regarding all aspects widely sought after. In this instance it is railway engineering.

5. The author uniquely combines the two distinct practices of medical and technical illustration in order to exemplify and promote the superior ergonomics afforded by this electric drill. The client was Atlas Copco Ergoline of Sweden.

6. Historic feats of engineering provide the technical illustrator with a conceptual opportunity to integrate hyperrealism with mechanical detail: John Fox elucidates the ubiquitous WW2 fighter aircraft 'Spitfire'.

4

Subject matter is multifarious and extremely diverse, from presenting an exposé of microchip-sized mechanics contained within a state of the art digital device to an intense and complete visual description of the structure and workings of an early 20th-century steam railway locomotive. It includes all vehicles of transportation, from spaceships to bicycles, architecture of all descriptions both historic and contemporary, instruments, artefacts, tools – the list is boundless.

As with aspects of scientific illustration the digital age has enabled this particular discipline to transcend new heights regarding visual language. The increase and demand for sophisticated and interactive learning and museum-based material, the emphasis placed on the quality of design and presentation regarding printed matter are reasons to suggest that the need to present technology-based information creatively and innovatively has never been greater.

5

6

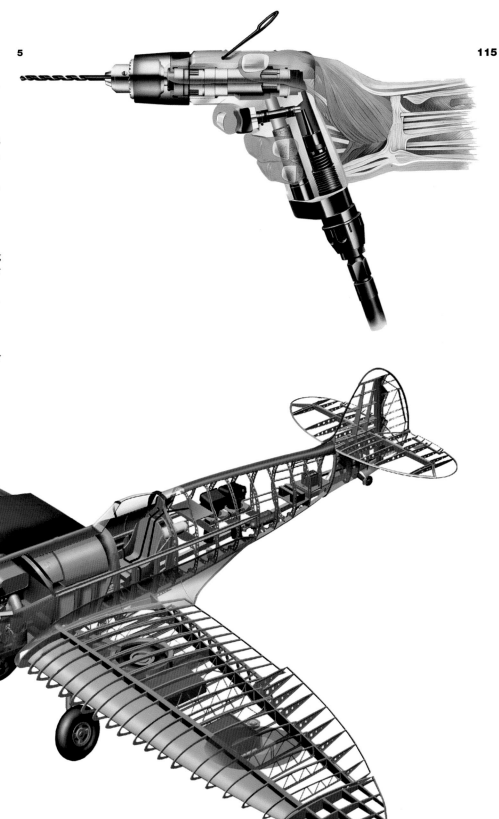

1

116 The Illustrator as Scientist and Cultural Historian

The notion of an illustrator assuming the professional status of scientist or cultural historian is not new. An example as shown by retail publishing is that there is an increase in the numbers of non-fiction children's books being authored and illustrated by the same individual. Why? What gives illustrators the right to uphold such 'upstart' positions of importance and authority?!

The status of the commercial art practitioner has increased in recent years with seemingly more responsibility for context and content. The graduate graphic designer will often be appointed as an art director soon after leaving higher education, whilst in times past it would have taken years of apprenticeship and gradual ascents in the promotional process. This may be a result of 'sea changes' in recent and current art and design undergraduate education. The reduction of an overtly vocational emphasis with subjects such as studio-based illustration practice now integrated with professional practice studies and contextual, historical and cultural studies has facilitated an educational experience enabling graduates to multitask, be professionally independent and to be much more intellectually capable. The best art and design undergraduate education encourages the acquisition of appropriate transferable skills that are not only practical, but intellectual and knowledge based: the command of written and oral language, presentation and research.

Professional and student illustrators undertaking research, commissioned and/or given project work will often be required to engage with specialist subject matter. This can often lead to the illustrator assuming a position of authority regarding one's thematic domain of operation. Continuous professional involvement with the topic, researching and illustrating books and other material at a national and international level would soon qualify the illustrator as an 'expert', even without a formal qualification in the subject. Opportunities to undertake focused postgraduate masters and research higher degrees can also facilitate and expand an illustrator's authorial status.

2

1. Roger Harris depicts expert knowledge regarding the aeronautics of space.

2–4. Paul Bowman combines illustration and an in-depth knowledge of contemporary history to convey comment regarding the Srebrenica atrocities during the Balkan conflict.

3

There are a number of scientific and cultural illustrators who trained specifically in subject matter; archaeology, botany, biology, zoology. These individuals have established their status of author/illustrator by approaching their education and training the 'other way round' by undertaking undergraduate science and cultural studies degrees first. In order to elucidate and 'illustrate' academic, practical or research work, certain individuals employ an inherent 'artistic gift' and thus begin to draw and visualise, initially as an aide memoir to their studies and then with later work manifesting as published texts with illustrations. All of this is exemplified by the roster of membership of the Guild of Natural Science Illustrators, a professional society with significant international standing. The intrinsic link between words and image, the increase in illustrators engaging directly with subject matter suggests the firm establishment of a culture representative of and given for the non-fiction author-illustrator.

4

'The best art and design undergraduate education encourages the acquisition of appropriate transferable skills that are not only practical, but intellectual and knowledge based: the command of written and oral language, presentation and research.'

1

118 Commentary

An Overview of Editorial Illustration

The essence of editorial illustration is visual commentary. Its principal function is to be symbiotic with journalism contained within the pages of newspapers and magazines.

This suggests that the potential for its use and breadth of application is vast. The media industry is extremely diverse covering a myriad of themes and topics; daily, weekly, monthly, periodical editions catering for general specific and niche markets.

Both historically and in a contemporary context, illustration has a significant presence within this aspect of publishing, even with competition from photography and an amount of 'waxing and waning' with regards to certain trends and fashions.

To review the industry that commissions and is representative of editorial illustration, one must first examine the world of newspapers.

As a whole, the newspaper market is a fairly typical embodiment of the societies it serves, particularly in the Western or 'free' world. It provides its readers and potential readers with editorial lines and stances, conducive with mainstream, and in some instances, not so mainstream, political beliefs and convictions.

There are 'quality' broadsheet newspapers, although not all in the United Kingdom subscribe to this papersize description; some have physically downsized with one in particular opting for the 'Berliner' format. Then there are the populist middle range and 'red top' tabloid editions.

Many broadsheets and tabloids publish 'colour supplements', magazines that accompany certain issues on a regular, often weekly, basis. These publications contain an array of commentaries, and 'lifestyle' articles that upon review, clearly benefit from the visual enrichment provided by an accompanying illustration. Some colour supplements and broadsheet newspapers in particular, adopt a serious and considered use for illustration with serialised articles featuring illustration on a regular basis.

2

1,3,5,6. Victuals, the source and preparation of, provides much editorial material for lifestyle magazines. Emma Dibben has produced energetic and evocative drawings for food-based articles.

2. Sarah Horne's energetic drawings for an editorial article entitled 'inside housing'.

4. Gemma Robinson has designed and illustrated an image that accompanies a commentary regarding the potential dangers of 'bird flu'. Conceptual and thought provoking this was commissioned for the 'Independent' newspaper.

3

With regards to magazines in general, there is evidence to suggest a dramatic increase in the number of titles and the subsequent circulation of many. A great number are 'household' names, having a substantial pedigree and reputation with a large national and international circulation to match. Others are either regional or narrowly focused. Some magazines are 'in house' for exclusive staff-employee readership, retail, manufacturing and service industries. There are magazines for the members of societies and trade unions, charities and trusts. Others are given free to the customer-travellers of airlines and rail companies. Popular, specialist and obscure themes and topics are covered: TV listings, health and fitness, cooking, women's and men's magazines, politics and economics, science and technology, computing, art, antiques, wildlife and nature, sports and pastimes from football to wargames, pet and animal appreciation from pig breeding to snail farming!

So why use editorial illustration and what exactly does it do? In the past, magazine illustration embodied both wistful sentimentality and optimistic romanticism in the form of painterly or hyperreal pictorial representations of people or other subjects generic with the published 'love stories' and 'tragi-real-life dramas' filling the pages of women's or lifestyle magazines. There was some respite in the form of humour and satire which manifested as 'political' cartoons or 'jokes'. At least there were assignations to opinion by way of social comment and observation.

Today, the best editorial illustration is thought provoking and contentious. Normally couched within the journalistic remit of political, economic and social commentary it challenges both popular and alternative opinion; it obfuscates and presents arguments; it poses questions and leaves them unanswered; it makes provocative statements; it also disregards aesthetics or notions of 'good taste' regarding subject matter or visual language; mark-making sometimes rendered with an objurgatory energy and bite!

4

5

6

1

120 There are other forms of editorial illustration that do not demand an approach that requires such an intense intellectual or conceptual engagement. Here, the requirement would be for a 'softer', more reposeful and composed delivery of opinion and comment; seasonal gardening tips, aspects of culinary practice, the best and worst insect repellents for the traveller, how to maintain a stress-free environment for your budgerigar! Whilst these examples of magazine articles may seem deficient in gravitas regarding journalistic thrust and comment, it nonetheless demands an approach by the illustrator to evoke either humour or a reasonable level of pointed opinion. The least challenging editorial illustration brief to undertake regarding any notion of serious commentary must be that of symbolic, semi-pictorial or abstract decoration. It would be interesting to predict or ascertain the number of horoscope pages to be published in the future that might contain totally original visual concepts representing this subject matter.

Magazines have traditionally been a forum for illustrators. In the past and probably to a certain extent today, illustrators are able to keep abreast of their peers, to observe what visual languages are most apparent and thus determine future developments regarding one's own style. The most prestigious magazines have often been seen as providing the illustrator with a yardstick for quality and reputation; to have one's work appearing on the pages of certain high circulation publications was to proclaim that you have now actually 'made it'. This premise can be likened to the actor 'treading the boards' at Stratford – prestigious, but un-lucrative. Nevertheless, there is exceptional professional value associated with editorial illustration even though most magazines have a constricted use and shelf life. The ever increasing range of daily and monthly publications bound by the scope of subject matter and journalistic reporting should ensure that there is no demise in the life blood of this domain of illustration practice.

2

1,4,5. Clementine Hope produced these images for 'The New York Times', a publication that extols and values the use of quality editorial illustration.

2. Stephen Lee works with satire and the craft of caricature. This image of Blair and the Law Lords was for Channel Four.

3. Louise Hilton: an editorial illustration to accompany an article about fashion.

6. John S. Cuneo is an exponent of wit and humour, this image being an example of a large proportion of work commissioned within the domain of editorial illustration: 'Is Al Green good for your sex life?'.

3

4

5

6

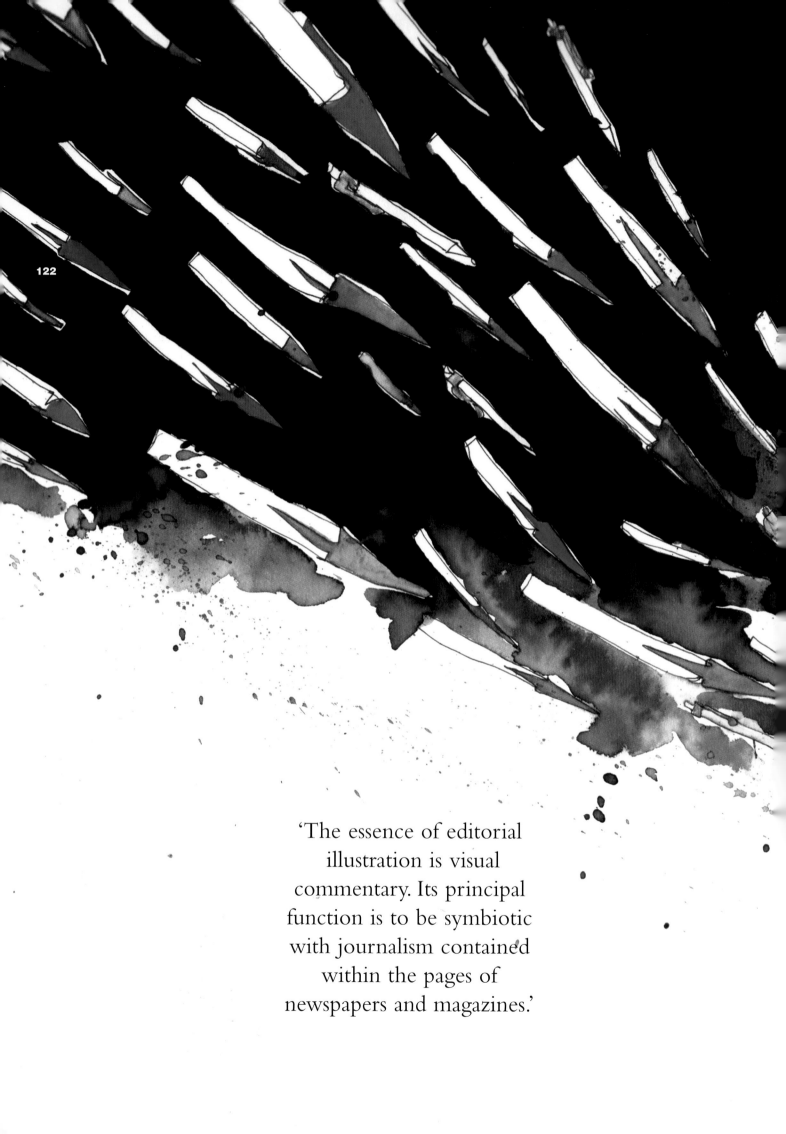

'The essence of editorial
illustration is visual
commentary. Its principal
function is to be symbiotic
with journalism contained
within the pages of
newspapers and magazines.'

1. Sarah Horne uses a comic approach to stereotype this character.

2. Humour is frequently infused into editorial illustration with a great many magazines given to entertain. This illustration by Beth Knowles chides the comment that '100 people every year choke to death on ballpoint pens'.

1

2

124

1

2

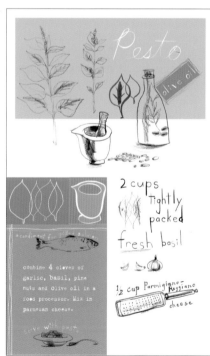

3

1. Reviews of popular television programmes provide much editorial material. This image by Lucy Truman describes destinations shown on 'Palin's Travels'.

2. The author introduces the 'Screaming Skull of Bettiscombe' for a travel article that recommends the best locations in Britain to experience the ghostly and the paranormal.

3. Recipes and the culinary arts feature extensively as editorial illustration. Ann Boyajian describes the ingredients and method to produce pesto.

4. Liz Lomax utilises best practice with these volumatic caricatures. The Presidents of the United States have provided an endless supply of material for the visual satirist: George W. Bush is no exception.

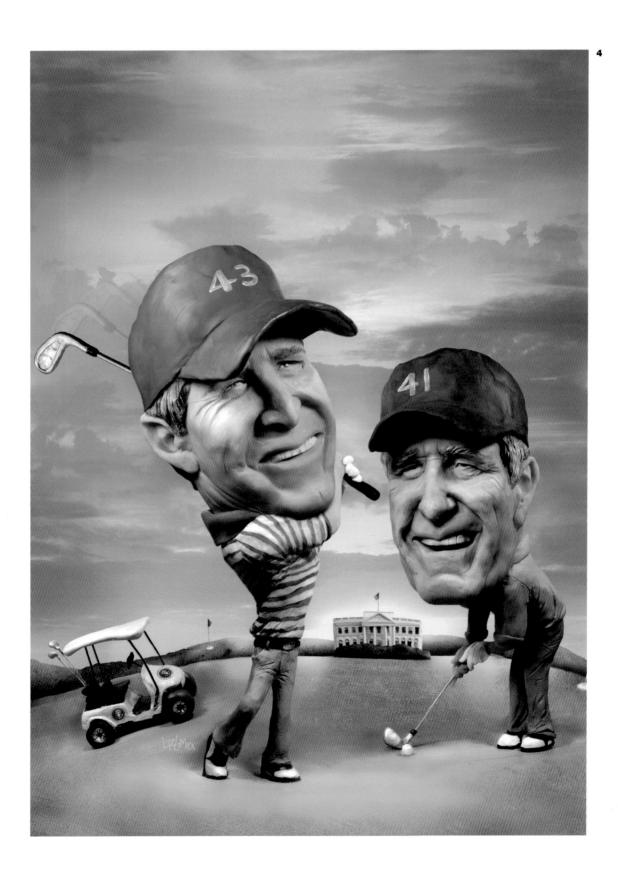

1

126 **Politics and Current Affairs**
The most abundant form of illustration
used editorially within most newspapers,
including those serving more regionalised
communities is that of the so-called
'political cartoon'.

Illustration of this genre has a distinguished
history. The culture of presenting virulent,
scurrilous and often libellous satire regarding
the deeds and personalities of contemporary
political leaders began as far back as the 15th
century. The advent and invention of the
printing press facilitated the mass production
and distribution of pamphlets, leaflets and
posters proclaiming, with some anonymity
from the writers, an array of political and
religious discontentments such as the
Protestant Reformation, The English Civil
War and other revolutionary concepts and
ideas. Firmly embedded within these textual
proclamations were woodcuts and other
'block' printed images, engravings that wildly
distorted truths in order to sway opinion.
These images also included depictions of
hated political and religious masters as
satanic and demonic, thus ensuring
maximum effect to the insult. The career of
the political cartoon had begun.

The 20th and 21st centuries have seen no
less regarding biting comment and lampoon-
ridden observations. However, because of the
establishment of democratic tradition and a
firmly embedded expectation to chide
and oppose government and political
philosophies of all persuasions, the
illustrators/cartoonists from the early 20th
century to the present day were and are
household names, synonymous with the
publications that employ them. So, how does
the best imagery of this genre work and
what makes it such an effective medium to
express comment and opinion?

An overview of this genre will reveal
representations of the human figure.
Sometimes the need is for a generic and/or
anonymous portrayal; a specific race, age group
or gender, distinctly formulated by action or
occupation and shown directly associated with
the issues being disclosed and discriminated.
These issues are often related to unpopular
political decisions affecting society, culture, the
economy, international diplomacy and conflict.

2

1. Political allies? The
antics of Blair and
Brown provide the
commentator with
much material, here the
pair are drawn by John
Bradley.

2,5. Stephen Lee
appropriates the
caricature to elucidate
editorial comment
ranging from highlighting
the certain character
traits and deficiencies
of media-inflated
personalities to political
satire.

3. A 'portrait' of the
former US Secretary of
State, Colin Powell by
Eivind Bøvor.

4,6. Owen Sherwood
has turned his attention
to so-called music
stars: M. Jackson and
M. Manson in receipt
of very little flattery.

3

More often than not it is specific individuals that invite hostility or ridicule pertinent to their 'recent actions'. Mostly politicians, but other media inflated personalities such as entertainers and sportspersons can expect no quarter from the pencils and pens of those illustrators contriving to humiliate, humble and mock!

It can be said that even those given to altruism, piety and self-sacrifice will succumb to laughing at the misfortunes of others; the bullying undertones, the insults and insinuations pointedly directed at the 'accused' by way of acid and 'on the edge' political cartooning.

The nature of this genre will reveal a style of illustration that encompasses a number of approaches. These can be symbolic, pictorial, humorous either in situation or deed, poignant, thought provoking and conceptual in message and visual language.

But the overriding character of this domain of illustration is the craft and practice of caricature. Varied approaches to visual language and autographic preference, and differential degrees of distortion provide for an area of practice that is extremely diverse. Sometimes a subtle change in a subject's physique or expression will push a portrait into a new realm of exposition. There can also be severe, almost 'violent' distortions applied to facial features. The degree and level of distortion is usually commensurate with the status and commentary being given regarding the subject's 'crime'.

4

5

6

'The overriding
character of this domain of illustration is the
craft and practice of caricature.'

1

128 Usually contentious in argument, the better illustrations of this nature satirise, amuse and sometimes shock. Past and present exponents include Bateman, Searle, Scarfe, Steadman, Hughes, Cummings, Mac, Bell, Adel, Payne, Luck and Flaw.

Working practices will vary. Newspaper cartoonists are often employed directly as staff and operate in-house. This can be advantageous to the practitioner because one can react instantly to a current affairs situation. The ideas and concepts are normally initiated and created by the illustrator who will be required to produce drawings immediately or overnight in order to comply with production schedules and publication routines.

This subject matter is firmly embedded within the context of editorial illustration. It is therefore prevalent to encounter caricatures and conceptual images on the covers and internal pages of national and international magazines: 'Time'; 'The Economist'; 'Der Speigal'; 'The New Statesman'; 'The Spectator'; 'Rolling Stone'; 'The New Yorker'. Caricatures have also been used in a three-dimensional format as puppets on television satire and comedy programmes.

Such is the insatiability engendered by the media for intrusion into the lives of the rich and famous, and for exposing their weaknesses and vulnerabilities – the craft of the caricature is here to stay. The pertinence of themes such as political opposition and propaganda, the increase in interest and knowledge related to global affairs suggest that all aspects of this domain of editorial illustration will continue to thrive.

2

3

4

5

1. Blair's New Labour cabinet 'appropriately' depicted as the 'Seven Dwarfs' by Richard Stanley.

2. The controversy surrounding HRH The Prince of Wales' second son (Prince Harry) regarding his 'regrettable and insensitive' choice of attire for a fancy dress party has provided Richard Stanley with an opportunity to further exacerbate the royal embarrassment.

3. John Bradley provides another expose of controversial policy associated with the Chancellor of the Exchequer.

4. Contemporary politics and the scandals befalling our elected representatives provide rich material for the current affairs illustrator. Here, Martin Wallace lampoons the 'activities' and 'lifestyles' that stigmatise senior figures in the British Liberal Democrat Party: the alleged alcoholism of leader Charles Kennedy and the 'rent boy' allegations associated with Simon Hughes and Mark Oaten.

5. Published in the 'Guardian' newspaper on September 11, 2006 this powerful image by Martin Rowson entitled '5 years on' offers telling and unnerving comment.

1

130   **'Lifestyle', Reviews and 'Bric-a-Brac'**
The broadsheet and middle range
newspapers and their associated colour
supplements are publications that often
feature specific columns given to review
and critique. Generally, these analyses and
judgements are filed against all aspects of
artistic practice: the opera, the stage, dance,
film, television, music, fiction, non-fiction
and the visual arts. Niche market magazines
will likewise proffer opinion and
considerations, detailing the appropriateness,
quality and commercial status if appropriate
of whatever 'state of the art' theme or subject
in question: motorcycles; vintage cars;
skateboards; guitars for the heavy metal
enthusiast; rare stamps; miniature laptop
computers; model soldiers; binoculars for bird
watching. This list is seemingly infinite.

However, if an illustration is required to
accompany and evoke important
observations regarding written commentary,
the illustrator must empathise with and
totally comprehend the thrust and essence of
the argument, no matter how populist and
distinguished, or obscure and minute the
opinions and subject matter might be. This
engagement is crucial if one is going to
provide a meaningful visual contribution to
the comments being expressed. Illustrations
that are integral with review and critique
must not be confused with imagery that is
commissioned to promote or advertise. A
fiction or non-fiction critique will deliver
an opinion related to quality. Even if this
particular critique is favourable opinion to
the narrative in question, the illustration is
neither to provide visual reinforcement to
the contents of the book nor package the
cover for retail and point of sale. The image
must elucidate the commentary.

2

3

4

1. Tom Frost presents
the usual choice
regarding moral
dilemmas.

2,3. Editorial reviews
are prevalent
commentaries that
critique and
occasionally lampoon.
Owen Sherwood
provides opinion
regarding 'Charlie and
the Chocolate Factory'
and 'Supersize Me'.

4. Sarah Horne
illustrates 'Soggy
Moggy'.

5,6. Rose Forshall
illuminates comment
made in 'The
Independent' regarding
the attitudes and mores
of wine tasting.

7. Tom Frost's editorial
illustration for 'The
Times Sex Page' hints
at the 'problems' being
analysed and
discussed.

5

Similarly, reviews related to other aspects of arts practice must also be approached accordingly. The illustrations should go far beyond a literal 'surface' definition of the topic; a photograph or attendance at a performance will provide more than adequate description. The image should be conceptual and thought provoking, perhaps containing elements seemingly unrelated to the main theme yet providing tangent, but alternative questions. The visual language should show that choices made regarding aesthetics or contents reflect the views of the commentator and the feelings evoked: an iconography appropriate for subjective yet considered emotions and reactions. Anger, disdain, joy, pleasure, excitement, sensuality and confusion are some of the expressive reactions that one must be able to convey through the creative use of illustration.

The domain of editorial illustration is exceedingly broad in respect of the subjects and topics encountered. Lifestyle is a generic term applied to all aspects of contemporary life: health and fitness; sex and relationships; cookery; hobbies and pastimes; DIY; fashion. The articles and commentaries associated with these can also be equally as diverse, particularly in terms of subject matter and seriousness.

6

7

1

132 Health and relationship issues often evoke a certain emotive intensity and gravitas regarding the nature of the article in question. Illustrations that accompany these articles should reflect an appropriate level of sensitivity and optimism.

There are also many published commentaries with illustration that do not offer much by way of intellectual engagement, but are in place to provide 'light relief', amusement and the occasional frisson: paranormal experiences; trends in tattoo design; teach yourself lycanthropy; how to live on a diet of rocks and soil; cooking and dining the aboriginal way – roast maggots for tea! Humorous yes, but also typical of the contents of a great many magazines.

The range of magazines available caters for an audience representative of all cultures, social status, occupations and moral opinion. This is an important contextual consideration to bear in mind and an understanding of one's target readership is crucial.

Sometimes, one is confronted with issues and questions related to personal ethics and morality. There is some material, particularly that couched in populism and trend that expresses values considered contrary to certain aspects of political correctness. Such is the diversity of opinion and topic divulged across the editorial divide, there will always be publications that certain individuals will be associated with.

2

1,3. Rebecca Riley apportions a recipe for the 'Long Island Iced Tea' cocktail.

2,4. Tom Frost's editorial illustrations represent the diversity of themes and commentaries that are worked with from investment masterclasses to fast food delivery.

3

1

134

To conclude, abstract or contradictory aspects of commentary can induce a much more innovative and experimental approach; one is conceptualising notions and elucidating material that comes from a fresh or totally original standpoint. To a degree, one has carte blanche to go beyond certain levels of expectation regarding conceptuality, visual language and expression. It is this aspect of editorial illustration that probably enables greater visual development regarding one's practice than any other contextual domain.

2

1. Jesse Mitchell comments about a previous century tax on hats.

2. John S. Cuneo demonstrates the best in humour with this editorial illustration for 'Esquire' magazine.

3. Eleanor Rudge exemplifies humour with an adult take on an editorial jibe at the quote 'you should try everything once, except incest and folk dancing'.

4. This editorial illustration by Nigel Owen comments on the eclecticism of restaurants and eateries that provide menus suitable for any time of the day or night.

3

4

1

136   **Illustrator as Journalist and Commentator**

Journalists write or broadcast reports and present commentary. Their field of operation is great and covers much from current affairs to specialist concerns. Can the work of certain illustrators be considered as journalism? Some illustration can certainly be considered as journalistic. Many illustrators attain specialist status with regards to subject matter and this can cross the divide of editorial practice. When producing an image in conjunction with a journalist writer, not only does the illustrator have the creative freedom to determine its essence, but should also pertain to knowledge and insight into the subject. Combined, the text and illustration presents opinion and account. In this context, the illustration is 'journalistic' in its nature.

But how can an illustrator replicate the work of a journalist? Many illustrators write professionally, both fiction and non-fiction material. However, in a contextual sense these examples fall into different domains of practice.

Can it be that illustration in itself can manifest as journalism? Photo-journalism certainly does. If photographic imagery can be evidenced as a form of journalistic practice, why not illustration? The art of drawing on location, visual note taking, is

2

3

1,2. Rose Forshall exemplifies reportage illustration with this editorial image entitled 'Borough Market'.

3. Vicki Behringer depicts the unfolding drama of the Michael Jackson trial by drawing directly from inside the actual courtroom. A meaningful and high-profile example of reportage illustration.

James Vinciguerra gives a sentient texture to these scenic visual interpretations. Borne out of direct and ambient connections with the locations in question this is reportage-style illustration at its best:
4. Mevagissey;
5. Radcliffe Square, Oxford;
6. Stratford Houses.

4

sometimes used as an alternative to photography, usually when the use of cameras is prohibited. Courtroom scenes are often recorded by an attendant illustrator, the imagery broadcast or published in newspapers. There is another field of practice whereby actual artwork is being commissioned. War artist/illustrators have been dispatched to areas of conflict in order to capture atmosphere and detail related to aspects of the unfolding history. Recent examples include the Falklands and the Balkans. In itself, this might be considered as adjacent to actual journalism as one could get. By their very nature and physical presence, the war drawings provide a 'hands-on' real-life experiential account of the dramatic events that they have recorded.

The term given for this method of practice is **reportage**: the illustrator working on location and visually recording appropriate aspects of the subjects covered. The illustrator David Gentleman is renowned for his reportage drawings and illustration normally produced on location in countries such as India; his books provide fascinating cultural insights and information.

Magazines and newspapers sometimes use reportage illustration for features about travel. The accent is on a 'rough guide' approach, provide visual commentary that tends to be 'warts and all'.

The illustrator can operate as a journalist. But one must transcend the role of being solely a visualiser and recorder of observed material. There needs to be a holistic approach that engenders status regarding one's authority and credibility with subject matter and working practice. It must also be said that the craft of writing is an essential component regarding the professional make-up of the journalist-illustrator. The boundaries of the media and creative disciplines are blurred. The essence and contextual thrust of writing and illustration is communication. Journalism with illustration is another example where this can be evidenced.

5

6

'Reportage: the illustrator working on location and visually recording appropriate aspects of the subjects covered.'

1

138   Storytelling

An Overview of Illustration for Narrative Fiction

It is often considered a prerequisite to provide visual representation of narrative fiction. This is a notion prevalent both historically and contemporaneously.

Throughout the ages, a great many people have been introduced to or influenced by so-called great works of art depicting literal or allegorical images associated with religion or the classics. At the behest of the early Christian church, tales from the Old and New Testaments have been translated into visual form exemplified by magnificent frescos, paintings and sculptures. There have also been dramatic reconstructions, sometimes manifesting as large sumptuous oil paintings of themes and scenarios from classic literature. Also, consider the large number of published volumes from the 19th century containing the many descriptive and atmospheric images by illustrator/engravers such as Tenniel, Cruikshank, Rackham and Beardsley. Historically, it would seem that art, and more laterally illustration, has provided an important visual exposition to the many myths, legends, anecdotes and fictitious events penned by the anonymous, the not-so-famous to the most revered of authors.

Today, narrative fictional illustration is mainly encountered in children's books, graphic novels and comic strips, and specialist publications such as thematic compilations, containing mythology, gothic tales and fantasy. Adult fiction in a contemporary context is probably the most under-represented genre regarding illustration either as an accompanying or intrinsic element. It has been said that 'the art is in the writing'. Commended written fiction not only maintains the reader's attention, but does well to describe and unfold the narrative whatever style or genre it is concerned with. The best will engender an emotional and imaginative engagement with the writing, whether classic or contemporary poetry, novel, romance or thriller.

2

3

1,4. David Young appropriately provides a pictorial image for this children's narrative entitled 'The Beachcombers'.

2. Michelle Thompson depicts a visually generic overview of 'The Loss of El Dorado'.

3. Levi Pinfold has created a simple, yet effective scenario depicting a group of figures interacting. This is for a book entitled 'We Wish', which contains a series of poems by young children.

4

140

However, publishers of adult fictional material will often call on the illustrator to provide suitable and appropriate imagery for the book cover. Contextually, this area of illustration practice must not be confused with narrative fiction, which is solely the domain of actual storytelling. The cover of a book functions as packaging and point of sale.

The craft of telling stories by using illustration is often sequential in form and essence. The nature of the imagery is dependent on fictional genre, style of writing and actual length. Imagery that is intrinsic with the story will often convey scenes of dramatic representation using the best practices of image construction; composition, effective and emotive use of colour, appropriate use of distortion and sense of space. The contents of the illustration should deliver visual intrigue, atmosphere and drama even if the scenario is passive in its nature, the full essence of the scene should be conveyed appropriately.

Many narratives operate with a substantial level of allegory with the abandonment of any direct literal association. In this instance there might be a description of a subject under the guise of another that has similarities to it, a picture in which meaning is symbolically represented. In this instance, the need to ascertain whether accompanying images should elucidate or be more enigmatic regarding the message is paramount to producing commendable narrative fiction illustration. The whole notion of combining words and pictures comes into play significantly here, the core essence regarding the telling of stories substantiated by the right balance of text and image.

1–4. Eivind Gulliksen imaginatively and humorously creates self-written fictional narratives, sometimes for an adult audience, always mindful of creating and using stylisation appropriate for characters and scenarios visualised and for the target audience.

5. Katy Wright provides an evocative visual accompaniment to the passage 'We can lift ourselves out of ignorance, we can find ourselves as creatures of excellence and intelligence and skill. We can be free! We can learn to fly.' 'Jonathan Livingston Seagull' by Richard Bach.

4

Finally, the context of narrative fiction has to be understood by its distinctiveness. In published form the contents and subject matter will conform as conventionally accepted falsehoods; everything is feigned, imagined or invented. As such, it is possible to 'go any place and do whatever thing'. This has a bearing on how an illustrator conceives imagery and how important credibility is in terms of represented reality. Some of the most creative and innovative illustration has been generated by way of this contextual domain. Its influence has had immense bearing regarding many aspects of published and performance entertainment, including animated films and motion pictures. Characters and events conceived and originated in their visual form by illustrators have given rise to many clichéd and accepted representations: Long John Silver, Bill Sikes, Superman, Snow White, Homer Simpson to name but a few. There is no doubt that the craft of illustration will continue with its important contribution to the world of 'make believe'.

'The whole notion of combining words and pictures comes into play significantly here, the core essence regarding the telling of stories substantiated by the right balance of text and image.'

5

142

1–4. Nick Hardcastle presents atmosphere and effective dramatic composition to elucidate the unfolding plotline for this series of 'Crime and Detective Stories'.

1

2

3

4

'Imagery that is
intrinsic with the story
will often convey scenes
of dramatic representation
using the best
practices of image
construction.'

1

144 **Picture Books and Early Readers**

The earliest appearance of illustration reproduced for young audiences was during the latter half of the 16th century. Produced as woodcuts these forerunners of what one might consider early children's book illustrations corresponded with the invention of printing and first appeared in Germany. At that time, the context seemed more to do with instruction and enlightenment rather than pure fictional narrative and it was not until the 19th century that children's book illustrations became synonymous with storytelling. It can also be considered a time when this particular genre blossomed and flourished in a manner not witnessed before. The advent of colour printing through the invention of lithography gave rise to a fresh, and for that period, innovative approach to image-making. The greatly improved processes of binding and manufacture provided consumers with books considered to be genuine quality products.

Influential publications from the 19th century include Edward Lear's 'A Book of Nonsense' containing black-and-white quasi surrealistic drawings that set a precedent being followed regarding humorous and ingenious imagery of this nature. In 1865 'Alice's Adventures in Wonderland' by Lewis Carroll was first published. Sir John Tenniel's illustrations became instantly recognisable and lauded as a byword for quality regarding this great children's story. Another important and influential children's book illustrator of the 19th century was Kate Greenaway. Her illustrations were evocative of the Victorian period with their adherence to the formalised social mores of the day with subjects being prissy in demeanour and engaged in innocent pursuits. These drawings were simplistic, line-rendered figurative representations and were amongst the first to benefit from colour printing. To conclude an overview of the 19th century one must consider the work of Randolph Caldecott. His illustrations comprised sophisticated scenes with figures interacting. They can also be considered as amongst the earliest not to literally convey the text, but elucidate the narrative as a whole making the words and pictures be truly symbiotic.

There was a Young Lady whose bonnet,
Came untied when the birds sate upon it;
But she said: 'I don't care!
All the birds in the air
Are welcome to sit on my bonnet!

2a

There was an Old Person of Hurst,
Who drank when he was not athirst;
When they said, 'You'll grw fatter,'
He answered, 'What matter?'
That globular Person of Hurst.

2b

There was an Old Man who said, 'Hush!
I perceive a young bird in this bush!'
When they said, 'Is it small?'
He replied, 'Not at all!
It is four times as big as the bush!'

2c

3

TOMMY was a silly boy,
" I can fly," he said ;
He started off, but very soon
He tumbled on his head.

His little sister Prue was there,
To see how he would do it ;
She knew that, after all his boast,
Full dearly Tom would rue it !

4

Illustrators from the 19th century:
2a–2c. Edward Lear's 'A Book of Nonsense' poems.
1,3–4. The pictorially evocative images of Kate Greenaway – some of the first illustrations in colour.

5

6

7

8

5–8. Randolph Caldecott, another successful illustrator from the 19th century whose images often 'shed new light' on to themes from the text providing additional and sometimes alternative insights into the narrative.

1

146 The early 20th century gave way to a sudden and rapid increase in children's book publishing with a great number of illustrators becoming synonymous with this genre; E.H. Shepard, Edmund Dulac, Beatrix Potter, and Edward Ardizzone. In the United States rich, full-colour images, painterly in style were setting new standards for children's books with illustrators such as N.C. Wyeth, Howard Pyle, Maxfield Parrish and Tom Lovell being amongst the protagonists of the time. They often provided a visual frisson to classic children's literature with dramatic and atmospheric reconstructions of adventures, intrigue and mystery.

However, from the 1950s onwards, the total dominance of pictorial representation, no matter how symbolic or metaphorical in essence, started to cede to a new and innovative approach to visual language. There transpired a more decorative and surreal character to methods of image construction. Some were influenced by early engravings or surface pattern designs, others by the new 'graphic design' of the day such as a utilisation of flat colour, abstract shapes and a minimalist working of space. But the overriding factor was that the contents, subject matter and intrinsic nature of the narrative fiction were overtly contemporary at the time. It was commonplace to see a changed and innovative representation of characterisation and vista with distortion and an unnerving juxtaposition of visual elements becoming the norm. A classical example of catalytic children's book illustration is 'Where the Wild Things Are' by Maurice Sendak. Published in 1963 these illustrations cannot be judged purely on visual language and character representation. They are indispensable to an understanding of the plot with expression and content depicted clearly within the pictures, often without words. This book and others of a similar genre and essence set a precedent for innovative and meaningful children's fictional illustration.

An examination of contemporary children's book illustration will reveal a multitudinous diversity of imagery and fictional genre. Many illustrators are 'household' names such as Quentin Blake, Michael Foreman and Richard Scarry. Indeed, many illustrators

2

3

4

5

6

1–6. Eivind Gulliksen has innovated with some good humour, creatures and other entities based on vegetables. These images are from a book he has written and illustrated entitled 'Spud the Nameless Potato'.

148 who are singularly associated with children's narrative fiction provide great influence and inspiration to many aspiring commercial artists. Because of the inventive possibilities afforded by the fantasy and imagination given to this field of practice, many visual communicators are attracted to its inherent creative outlet.

Such is the diversity of cultural association and influence exposed to young audiences today by way of content and visual language, it is impossible to focus on any one genre that might be considered fashionable. Disneyesque characters, plots and scenarios still prevail with lightweight sentimentality and a banal approach to entertainment, as opposed to what might be considered its antithesis: the European approach. This embodies a much deeper and more sensitive working with subject matter and narrative. Some are borne out of the Hans Christian Andersen tradition and will evoke emotive themes demanding a certain gravitas in its status.

Illustrators who work within this domain, particularly those from Eastern Europe, are unafraid of themes or issues related to human suffering or desire. Approached with a sensitive and appropriate visual treatment such as an economy of explicitness, the needs of the intended age group are paramount. This brings to attention the essential requirement for an understanding of one's given audience. In order to fully comprehend these fundamentals it might be expedient to examine the different age groups and an overview of the types of publication associated with each age group:

Six months to two years:
interactive books such as floating bath and board, 'shape' books all with simple text, adult narrated.

Two years to five years:
picture books, 'pop-ups' and novelties with early reader text.

Five years to eight years:
chapter books – picture books of a more sophisticated nature with associated text.

Eight years to twelve years: first novels.

Twelve years +: young adult material.

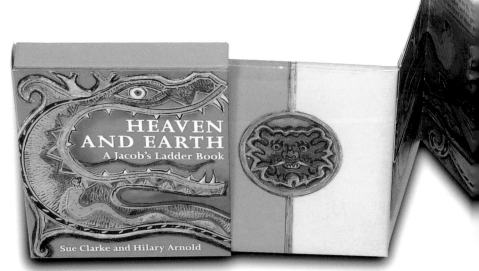

1,2. Considered by some as narrative fiction, texts from the Bible are often described as a collection of parables and metaphorical interpretations. However, Bible stories for children provide a rich source of material for the illustrator, as shown in these images by Judy Stevens.

3,4. Sue Clarke exemplifies an innovative approach to presenting Bible stories with this evocative and visually rich interpretation, boxed and manifesting as an interactive 'pull-out'.

4

'An examination of contemporary children's book illustration will reveal a multitudinous diversity of imagery and fictional genre.'

1

150 It is apparent from this simple taxonomy that there are considerable differences regarding general age range, attainment, ability and potential needs. Any children's book will conform to one of these descriptions.

The following questions are essential: Does the intended publication have a specific target audience with defined learning needs? Is there a broad cultural or ethnic diversity envisaged or is the readership specific or parochial? What curriculum or school grade is associated with the age group and what skills are they expected to master? In a generalised sense what are their level of motor skills? What might their interests be? Consider a gender balance and recollect one's own interests and inquisitiveness at that particular age.

The definition of a 'picture book' would suggest a publication for very young children with an approximate age range from two to five years. The illustrations will play a role as important as or even more important than the text. 'Chapter books' are generally longer and for older children, approximately five to eight years and who are learning or have just learned to read. These publications contain more sophisticated subject matter, treatment and language.

So, what are the intellectual and practical processes associated with illustrating and if appropriate writing a complete children's book of this nature?

Before commencement, there are questions regarding the design and visual concept of the book. If one is commissioned to undertake this project then the publication in question might be part of a thematic series, such as a compilation or 'boxed set' by the same author and therefore might be subjected to an already established house style with corresponding size, typography and graphic layout. As the illustrator, does one have free rein

5

That's when my Friend George visits me.

Sometimes he's

GIGANTIC

But mostly he's just big

2

Now I can see all sorts of things happening
I see huge worms racing each other in grand tunnels
I see scary fish in underground seas
And behind us, I see angry rabbits filling in our hole.

3

Before long we are miles through the ground.
Soon I can't see the top of the hole any more
and it gets dark

So George turns his lights on.

4

6

I was sitting in my Garden
On one sunny afternoon

7

2–5. Juan Moore has created a fantastical character for his self-penned young audience story entitled 'Gigantic'. The representation of the main character does well not to go beyond the boundaries of acceptability with regards to the way a child might perceive a potential frightening entity.

1,6–7. Sarah Nayler provides a contemporary visual language and characterisation that would not be misplaced in another contextual domain such as commentary or persuasion.

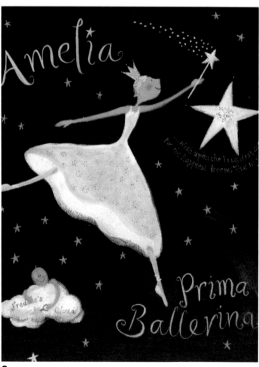

1

152 regarding the size of the book and number of pages? Unless the publication is specifically large, such as an anthology of stories, it is normal for picture books and chapter books to comprise single signature bindings of 16, 24 or 32 pages. The majority of chapter books in particular conform to the standard 32-page format. After the title page, publisher's information and data page have been taken into consideration there would be 12 to 13 'working' double-page spreads given to express through pictures and words the complete fictional narrative. It is essential to know and comply with these precepts before the commencement of any creative or visual work.

If one is to establish a role as both author and illustrator, particularly of picture books and chapter books, then the creation of the setting, plot and characters can be borne out of the drawing process. However, one cannot invent a fictional narrative 'out of thin air'. There has to be inspiration or a desire to undertake this bidding. It is much more advantageous to proceed with a topic that holds a strong, personal interest. This can make the subject unique and confers it with animate bearing.

One should also empathise with the setting of the story. Unfamiliarity with a setting that is appropriated by one's readers can destroy credibility. Each setting has unique advantages and disadvantages and it is important that all is completely understood. If the setting is periodic, one must ensure that the facts surrounding it are correct. A contemporary setting should provide a backdrop for one's characters to think and know in a way the present day young audience would. Each generation has a 'language', even a culture of its own and whereas basic human nature does not change, customs, fashions and mores do.

The favourable development and outcome of one's characters is paramount to the successful creation of children's narrative fiction. A guiding principle is to ensure that the characters are believable to oneself. If this can be attained then it is very possible for them to be real or credible to the readers. It is also important to ensure that they do not act 'out of character'. One cannot

2

1,2. Asa Andersson illuminates the letters of the alphabet in a traditional yet appropriate style forever mindful of the target audience and the educative underpinning of the concept.

3. Jo Goodberry provides illustrations that have stylised figure characterisations yet are realistically credible in pose and movement, clearly borne out of objective, observational drawing.

4,5. Yannick Robert's illustrations for 'King of Spring', a traditionally humorous and imaginative tale with all characters and scenarios appropriately designed to complement and enhance the text.

3

After that, the King of Spring bounced everywhere. He had the ceiling in the castle repaired so no-one could bounce through it. He brought back the balls and the balloons and all the bouncy things. And he made a new VERY IMPORTANT LAW: every week the people had to go to the Castle meadow and see the lambs. That way, they would be sure to keep on bouncing.

4

Now when the King bounced into the attic something strange happened. A nasty November gremlin had grabbed him, and was sitting on his shoulder.

"Call yourself a king?" whispered the gremlin. "Kings are sensible and wise, not silly, bouncy fools. You must never, ever bounce again." At that, a small tear rolled down the King of Spring's face.

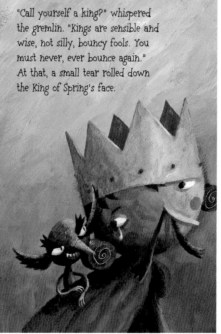

5

1

154 successfully maintain credibility with characters if they are manipulated to behave in a manner they would not do so in reality. Reference must be made to how an individual has been developed in terms of their personality and disposition, their appearance, family and peer situation.

Whatever visual language employed from caricature, distortion or representationalism, every character must be conceived from painstaking observations of body language, gesture, expression, movement, individual idiosyncrasy and eccentricity. Accurate visual studies of this nature can be pushed into whatever exaggerated or realistic poses necessary to make the character 'do' what is required.

Personality, trait and emotion must also be convincingly portrayed. Mood and sense of being can be presented by an appropriate representation of physical gait, hands and facial expression.

There is also the question of what is acceptable for presentation to young audiences. This particular domain of practice has over the years provided illustrators with immense scope to 'push the boundaries' regarding the conception and visualisation of 'extreme characters': monsters, ghouls, ogres, witches and many other frightening entities that have pervaded the pages of children's literature. However, there are often editorial checks and balances regarding content and how it is visualised. Much of this is related to the main characters within the plot. It would seem that an essential ingredient to infuse into one's characters is 'appeal'. Stylised and distorted facial features must not perceive a character to be unpleasant or threatening. The size, shape and placement of the eyes, nose and mouth are all important considerations.

The representation of animals and their subsequent characterisation is also an important aspect of children's narrative fiction. Here, the process of character conception and visual development is the same as before. However, because of the diversity of species within the animal

2   **3**

4   **5**

6

7

1,8–9. Jamie Smith avoids direct anthropomorphism and opts for a 'user friendly' approach to animal representation with characterisations that

could be used several times over in books and other contexts.

Linda Scott uses narrative-based imagery to engage a young audience with an empathetic understanding of moral and social issues: **2–5.**

The four smaller illustrations deal with themes of religion; temptation and the message underpinning Jonah and the Whale: **6,7.** Bullying and race.

8

9

'The favourable
development and outcome
of one's characters is
paramount to the successful
creation of children's
narrative fiction.'

1

156 kingdom and the scope for distinctly different stylistic approaches, this area can provide immense creative and inventive opportunities. The animals 'play-out' scenarios that are either fantastical or a replication of reality associated with the broad sphere of humanity.

Over the years, animals have been portrayed to be both good and evil with certain species stereotyped as one or the other. The visual representation can vary from the 'twee' to the contemporaneously challenging; familiar 'fluffy' domestic creatures to outrageously distorted invertebrate monsters. Anthromorphism is a method of stylisation that has been utilised for centuries. Ever since the early East European woodcuts and engravings depicted legendary lycanthropes, Beatrix Potter's rabbits and friends along with Bestall's Rupert Bear have given animals distinct human physical characteristics, almost to the point of being people with animals' heads. This way of character development is still much considered and used today. However, one must also recall the importance of audience perception and receptivity. Animals as substitute children within a narrative, often in anthromorphised form will engage the audience with empathy and imagination.

With regards to the plot, it is essential to know where one is proceeding and to firmly establish, for example, how the mystery is going to be solved at its conclusion and as the narrative unfolds how seemingly impracticable barriers are overcome throughout. If the conceived narrative is fantasy it is important to abide by the laws that one's fantasy dictates. There is nothing in fantasy to suggest that a 'miracle' will ensure that everything will 'turn out okay' because the world of one's story is imaginary; classic fairy and folk tales are based in actuality and the events and their outcomes abide by the strictures of credible reality. It is too easy to concoct a story that is 'far-fetched'.

Textual and visual dialogue and interaction are key aspects of maintaining an appropriate pace and flow throughout the book. This immediately alludes to the important relationship between words and imagery.

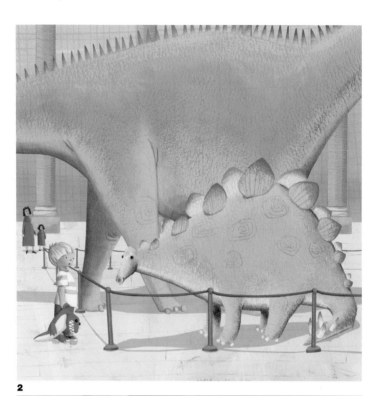

2

3

Mandy Field's human and animal characterisations are conceived and rendered with an animate and distinct stylisation, but are nonetheless borne out of solid, academic drawing practice. The observation and scrutiny of elements such as gesture, form and movement helps to give the figures their character and credibility.
1. Is entitled 'Habb'.
2. Is a cover illustration for a story called 'Dinosaur'.
3. Is from 'Rumplestiltskin'.

4,5. Kosei Kawakubo utilises collage and surreal juxtapositions as opposed to pictorial 'real space' with this illustration for a book of poems by young children entitled 'We Wish'.

4

These two elements should articulate in a simultaneous manner, without duplication and be complementary to one another. An example might provide for a component of surprise, the imagery depicting one suggestion or direction, the words alluding to something completely different or unseen, furnishing questions, subtle nuances and twists to the underlying message contained in the illustration.

Before embarking on the actual process of designing and illustrating the book, it is appropriate to produce a synopsis of the project. This can provide a potential client or publisher with an overview in order to consider its feasibility. The synopsis should include: a working title; an order of contents; a full description of the narrative plot, its characters, the beginning, middle and conclusion including a moral sub-plot if appropriate; a rationale, its inspiration, intended audience and potential marketability. It is also appropriate to produce or provide a speculative artwork that shows the intended visual language and treatment. It should be an image that relates directly to the book. It should also depict a significant scenario from the narrative with a clear visual indication of the main characters and is intended for inclusion in the book.

Illustrating narrative fiction for young audiences is often regarded as a primary exhibit. Even if one is not the author or originator of the publication, by undertaking its visual essence and design, the cover and all images contained within provides the illustrator with an important showcase.

157

'Textual and visual dialogue and interaction are key aspects of maintaining an appropriate pace and flow throughout the book.'

5

1

158   **Comics**

As a narrative fictional genre, the comic strip
has been and is ubiquitous throughout the
world. It is also a format that has not
changed very much and appears well placed
to continue in its current form. But what
defines a comic strip?

It can be said that a comic portrays a story
through a series of sequential illustrations.
The narrative may be humorous or satirical.
It can present a diverse array of narrative
genre from gothic horror, adventure, science
fiction, historical or period drama to
mystery, crime and fantasy.

Its audience is equally diverse from the very
young to adult specialist aficionados of
obscure graphic novels. Another defining
feature is that it often presents regularly
recurring characters by continuation from
one issue to the next over a period of time.
Although not always the case – some comic
books are single issue – the majority
conform to weekly, monthly or some other
defined periodic publication date. The
inclusion of the 'word balloon' for text is a
graphic styling rarely seen elsewhere within
the domain of visual communication. It is a
feature that provides the comic with its
particular mark. The visual language
employed ranges from hyperrealism to
extreme stylised realism often utilising the
drawn line technique accompanied by a bold
use of tone and shadow. Normally figurative,
the emphasis is much to do with creating
dramatic effect, a storyboard film direction
approach with due consideration for all
elements of pace, suspense and rhythm. The
dialogue presented in a manner similar to
live-action drama, with the word balloons
providing a direct correlation with the
unfolding story. The comic strip is the
presentation of narrative fiction given over
to almost pure drawn illustration.

1

2

1–4. This
contemporary 'comic
strip' by Erik Wayne
Patterson, entitled
'If/Then' relies on
minimal text and
creates the unfolding
narrative by utilising a
simplistic yet informal
approach to layout and
visual language.

3

What is the history of the comic strip and where and when did it begin? While sequentially arranged pictures may have a millennia-long formal history, the comic strip has a more specific past and origination. Hand-drawn illustrations appeared regularly in newspapers and magazines starting in the early 19th century. Many of them used humorous or unflattering portrayals of celebrities and were the origin of contemporary cartoons and comics.

The instant cited by historians of the comic strip as the moment of the form's origin was the publication in the United States of Richard Felton Outcault's 'The Yellow Kid', which appeared in the 'Hearst New York American' in 1896. It was published in the Sunday supplement to that particular newspaper and was soon to be joined by other comic strips. Outcault departed from the single-panel format and drew his trademark character in a series of panels. It also conformed to the overall definition of comic strip; visual sequence and published recurrence with a regular featuring of the individualised character.

During the early part of the 20th century, the 'Sunday comics' had become extremely popular in the United States. The newspaper publishers of these supplements would often present for retail small books containing reprints of past strips. The genre of the comic strip had become firmly established.

2

4

1

160 By the late 1930s, many of the now-famous superheroes made their first appearances in comic books, and the sales of these publications soared as 'good triumphed over evil'. Characters such as Batman, Superman and Spiderman are as popular today as in yesteryear with Hollywood being a particular beneficiary.

In Britain, 14 April 1950 witnessed the birth of a landmark comic; 'The Eagle'. This publication presented fresh standards in format, design and visual quality, the 'Dan Dare' drawings of Frank Hampson setting the established criteria for judging the highest levels of draughtsmanship and overall illustrative excellence.

However, the contents of many British comics from that post Second World War period adopted certain 'end of empire' jingoistic aspects and attitudes. Often, male-gender-specific publications would feature characters such as the Second World War spitfire ace 'Paddy Payne: Warrior of the Skies' outrageously wreaking deadly havoc upon the enemy. Today, the contents of comic books are still considered 'questionable' by certain quarters; moral and ethical issues related to explicit levels of violence and sex are often cited when

2

'Normally figurative, the emphasis is much to do with creating dramatic effect, a storyboard film-direction approach with due consideration for all elements of pace, suspense and rhythm.'

1,2. Tom Gauld's visual sequence entitled 'Hill Top' utilises the comic strip boxed-panel format without the need for textual inclusion.

3–5. One of the most popular 'comics' sold throughout the United Kingdom contains strictly adult material and has a total disregard for political

correctness. 'Viz' lampoons social stereotypes and major aspects of British society as exemplified here by Graham Dury's 'Fat Slags'.

debating the justification for the continued existence of this genre of illustration practice. Nonetheless, some publications have assured cult status and are marketed as containing distinctly adult material. The British publication 'Viz' has utilised the comic strip format to present a regular series of 'situation comedies' that lampoon and satirise all aspects of society. The graphic novel has assumed new heights of popularity with illustrators such as Dave McKean being an exceptional proponent. Comics for very young audiences still provide trite and insignificant entertainment with 'Disneyesque' and 'Manga-like' stylisation.

Also today, there are comic publications associated with special interest groups and sub-cultures. There are regular national and international conventions specifically given for individuals to present, exchange or sell new comic book material initiated and produced by themselves. Such is the popularity of this domain of illustration and form of publication it is a practice of visual communication that cannot be ignored.

161

1

162 **The Illustrator as Author of Fiction**

Narrative fiction is undoubtedly the contextual domain of practice that offers illustrators the most significant opportunities for authorship. Approximately 50 per cent of young audience fiction is both written and illustrated by the same individual. The graphic novel and other sequential forms provide further opportunities. The suggestion here is that one assumes a dual role: illustrator and writer. However, when engaged with the dual disciplinary practice of illustration and authorship, how does one deal with the balance regarding text and image and which takes precedence? As an illustrator, it may be difficult not to allow the visual aspect to assume a significant presence. In practice the majority of cases show that one's audience connects with the perceived narrative by engagement with and elucidation by a sequence of illustrations accompanied by a relatively small amount of text that interacts simultaneously and corroborates either succinctly or literally the message given through the images. Examples of this form of practice are exemplified by word balloons in comics and the concise sentences and paragraphs contained in children's picture books. Here, the illustrator is conceiving an imaginary tale which is original in terms of authorship. But is the intention for it to be renowned for high standards in creative writing? One is embarking on an inventive and innovative process that manifests in published form therefore the written aspect should match the illustrations in terms of standards and professional acceptability, even if the words are seen as an accompanying entity to the imagery.

Initially, one's ownership, personal expression and choices made as creator and author can be given precedence over any notions of being commissioned in a standard commercial manner. This is where a publisher merely oversees the production of prescribed and heavily art directed images. Any form of narrative fiction conceived by an author–illustrator, whatever mould envisaged for publication, will generally manifest as an entity comprising text and image. However, it is the content and essence of the invented story, its plot and setting that is of paramount importance.

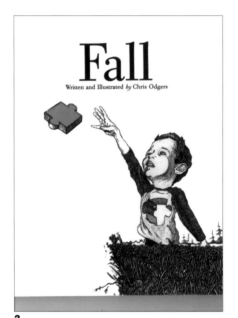

2

3

1,2,4,5. Chris Odgers works within a niche of narrative fiction suited to a broad audience, including adults. He specifically writes and illustrates books that have a limited print run, whereby they acquire collectable edition status. The illustrations and text (written in verse) exemplify best practice in picture and word symbiosis.

3. The children's picture book is a medium that provides the most opportunities for illustrators to combine with authorship. This is the cover of 'Marvin Wanted More' written and illustrated by Joseph Theobald.

4

It has been said previously that the conception of fictional narrative is a process that can allow one's imagination and creativity to 'fly' free and unhampered. But it is important not to lose sight of one's strengths and limitations regarding interests, inherent general and specific knowledge and sources of inspiration. These are factors that can initiate and facilitate a 'spark' of ideas and concepts for a potential story.

The working practice of author-illustrator has professional status, but one is rarely commissioned to produce a self-written and illustrated fictional narrative. Therefore, one has complete uninhibited freedom to create. It is also necessary not to feel compelled to pursue a theme, plotline or genre seemingly dictated by contemporary fashion or trend. The most original and challenging stories often 'buck the trend'.

Whatever one's particular interests and aspirations, it is fundamental to know and understand the parameters and distinctiveness of fictional genre and the possibilities afforded regarding one's own practice. This also includes an awareness of one's audience potential and appropriate media and publishing outlets.

163

'The conception of fictional narrative is a process that can allow one's imagination and creativity to "fly" free and unhampered.'

5

1

164   Persuasion

Advertising Illustration in Practice

The contextual domain most associated with pure commercialism is that of the world of advertising. It is also the most prescribed and directed form of illustration practice. But in a professional sense, it can also potentially provide the illustrator with the highest fees, particularly if the client and brand being sold has a high profile status.

However, the negative aspects regarding this way of working are exemplified by inhibited creative freedom; advertising agency art directors and copywriters usually initiate and devise the concepts for the campaign. This implies that an illustrator is selected and employed solely for one's visual language and proven dedication and adherence to the punishing schedules and deadlines expected. One must also be prepared to embrace, even if only temporarily for the duration of the commission, the culture and attitudes that prevail throughout this sector. There can be a 'hard edged' and unsentimental approach to working practice; indeed it has been described as a 'brutal environment'.

Also, the advertising world does not always distinguish between what many might consider 'good or bad taste'. The audiences and potential customers 'played to' by way of advertising campaigns are categorised in a somewhat crude taxonomy that identifies certain people's social status. This can often be gender specific, is sometimes based on regionality and one's placement within the scale of hierarchy determined by wealth (or lack of wealth). It has to be said that the vast majority of advertisers operate with integrity and do not deliberately set out to offend; on the contrary, the overriding objective is to 'sell'. However, it might be that the illustrator has to confront certain questions of conscience or morality in relation to the

2

3

4

1. Emma Dibben's seemingly animated 'still life' promotes a particular brand of continental lager.

2,3,5. Jonathan Burton's surreal images provide an entertaining and colourful concept to promote and sell a certain model of motor car.

4. Mark Hess uses the craft of pastiche to some effect with this advertisement for a particular brand of spaghetti sauce.

6. David Young uses a 'tried and tested' theme and visual pastiche for this campaign to promote teacher recruitment.

5

thrust of a campaign associated with a potential commission: it may be considered that a certain product or service is in some way destructive to the environment; there may be an issue related to animal welfare, religion or some other question of ethical concern. With regards to visual language and any conceptual input that might be expected of the illustrator, the level and degree of art direction will depend largely on the theme and essence of the original ideas initiated by the agency creative team. An illustrator with a particular working knowledge of a subject or topic that is the main feature of the campaign may be expected to develop the concept in a visual sense and be given freedom associated with the design and composition of the image; the placement of elements within space and the levels of abstraction and visual contortion. As an illustrator, one would have been selected for style and there would be an expectation to remain within the parameters of that style, irrespective of one's own ideas about the overall concept.

Another negligible issue related to strict adherence with visual language is that one might be required to produce a pastiche or a direct imitation, particularly if one's style and technique matches an appropriate original. An example is where the American illustrator Mark Hess was commissioned to provide a near identical replica of the Mona Lisa, except that the figure is made to appear dramatically overweight compared to the original. The advertisement, for a spaghetti sauce contained the appropriate caption, 'chunky'.

6

'As an illustrator, one would have been selected for style and there would be an expectation to remain within the parameters of that style, irrespective of one's own ideas about the overall concept.'

166   In spite of these negatives, many illustrators are able to create exemplary and innovative visual solutions, conceived, designed and worked to the highest standards of contemporary illustration practice. Indeed, it is one of the disciplines recognised and lauded by way of annual awards given for excellence in illustration for advertising. The Design and Art Directors Club of Great Britain, The Society of Illustrators and Communication Arts are professional organisations providing opportunity for recognition in this way.

The diversity of visual language employed is vast. There is no particular trend or house style associated with the broad church that is advertising. Campaigns will use styles that evoke whatever is necessary to facilitate the imparting of the 'right message', from 'chocolate box' to 'shock'; decorative, whimsical and historical stylisation; humour and caricature; 'hard-edged' technological and contemporary visualisation.

Potential exposure for the illustrator is equally diverse and overtly within the public domain: 'outdoor media' – bus shelters and bus sides, roadside billboards, railway and underground stations; 'on-air media' – television, cinema and online advertising; newspapers and magazines.

2

1–3. Alcoholic drink provides the advertising creative with much scope to initiate entertaining and innovative campaigns – mainly because there is nothing to say or laud about the products (except alcoholic potency perhaps). Laurence Whiteley gives cultural flavour to these well-known beers.

4. Brian Grimwood humorously suggests using the underground in order to visit London Zoo.

5. Rafal Olbinski's Society of Illustrators Gold Award for best use of illustration in advertising. The performing arts provide much work for illustrators.

This is no exception with Olbinski utilising his trademark surrealism to excellent and telling effect.

3

4

5

1

168 **Promotion and the Essence of Advertising**

The power of persuasion cannot be underestimated and illustration has throughout the years contributed enormously to this precept.

Advertising illustration or 'commercial art' first appeared as black-and-white line drawings in newspapers and was principally used as flattering visual representations of household products and effects, toiletries and fashion. Today, if illustration is chosen as part of a campaign, whatever its nature, the intention will be for it to aid the imprinting of brand recognition and awareness into the subconscious of society at large. Such is the power of this command that there are examples where illustration has not only been effective in product identity and persuasion, but has also contributed to a massive cultural vicissitude.

The early appearance of Father Christmas in his current guise is one such example. The illustrator chosen by the Coca-Cola Company in the 1930s to visually 're-invent' Santa Claus as a benevolent white-bearded man attired in brand colours almost to the point of replicating a bottle of the said drink, was undoubtedly unaware of the impact he was about to unleash on an unsuspecting Western society. The rest is history.

The overriding aim of the advertising industry is to sell and promote whatever product, idea, service or entertainment at their clients' behest. This implies that a vast diversity of campaign strategies and ideas are utilised, from the direct marketing and selling of items and services, to the use of propaganda and persuasion for political purposes. The diversity and extent of conflicting interests and beliefs that manifest from advertising campaigns and promotional strategies can sometimes present the illustrator with either ethical dilemmas or vague bemusement, depending on one's personal stance. An example is where the author was commissioned by a well-known manufacturer of agricultural pesticides to produce a realistic representation of a common rat, but to distort the features in a manner that rendered the creature as most

2,3. The author confronted with ethical dilemmas through the concept of 'Superbug', a chimeric combination of agriculturally destructive arthropods to promote the sale of insecticide. Also a visually distorted rat conveying its worst features: 'Send him off with a good square meal inside him'.

4,5. A concert of music based on themes of political revolution to be performed at the Royal Festival Hall provides Laurence Whiteley with the scope to produce bold and appropriately evocative imagery for this poster.

1,6. Alasdair Bright has conceived a humorous scenario that incorporates some 'unlikely' characters for this business trade press advertisement.

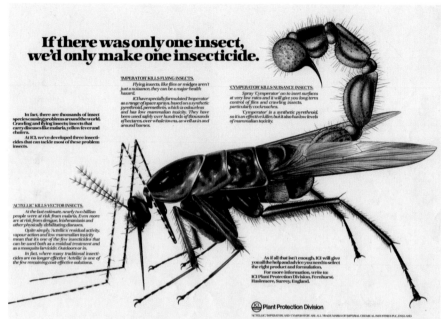

2

3

4

undesirable and deserving of the 'good square meal' of poison intended for it! The 'antidote' commission came soon after. An environmental pressure group of international standing also required a realistic rendition of a common rat but with a softer and more sentimentalised treatment so as to engender sympathy and endearment for the creature. The campaign was to promote the protection of its habitat.

The use of illustration has been a powerful tool in propaganda and the promotion of political ideology. The 20th century witnessed massive upheavals through world wars and bloody revolutions. The strength and power of the imagery used to desecrate, humiliate and promote the destruction of political opponents and specific ethnic groups is frighteningly apparent by fact of history.

Today, political parties and groupings utilise all methods of propaganda and persuasive techniques to extend their messages and it is the advertising industry that facilitates this. It may be fortunate, in the eyes of many that the majority of illustrations commissioned for promotional purposes works with material far beyond any connection with politics. A glance through the awards and promotional pages of illustrators' annuals will reveal an overwhelming presence of illustration used to promote the stage and theatre; opera and ballet, music, culture, arts festivals and events, musical performances and concerts, and specific venues such as jazz clubs and exhibitions.

Perhaps the inherent connection that illustration has with arts and culture suggests a reasonable justification for its use in this context. Most artistic and cultural genres would be best served by imagery that is constructed with aesthetic sensibility and visual intelligence. The major aspect of advertising is to promote the sale of products for the consumer. Any physical entity or service provision intended for sale or hire could be included on a list of 'products' that would be seemingly infinite. A broad and generalised list may suggest the following:

5

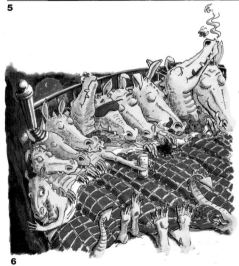

6

1

170 food and drink; personal effects; clothing; household and workplace utilities; furniture and appliances; vehicles; communications, media and technology; power; travel and vacation; financial services; private and public services. Many advertising campaigns will use elements of entertainment and humour with certain television commercials ceding to levels of situation comedy and farce. The use of illustration to convey amusement and facetiousness through advertising is no exception. A typical example is a comic representation of Noah's Ark at rest on the top of Mount Ararat, with humorous and characterful animals all around, paired off and in copulatory pose. The client was a dating agency.

All illustration used within this contextual domain must be intrinsic with the direct and successful transfer of positive messages related to promotion and sales. If not, then the image is rendered invalid. The illustrator cannot be sidetracked or distracted by a desire to 'go elsewhere'. It has been said that there is no place in advertising for illustrators who are 'precious and act like prima donnas'. A focused and direct approach is essential. One must be mindful of the intended audience, the illustration complementary to a message that ensures an appropriate level of cultural sensibility and sophistication. There is a natural desire by many illustrators to assume responsibility for the creative and overall conceptual elements related to an advertising campaign. The working processes of illustration practice related to other contexts of operation afford significantly more creative and conceptual freedom. Therefore this particular desire ought to be assumed a reasonable ambition. We have author-illustrators and illustrators who are experts in certain subjects. Perhaps in the future, as illustrators are afforded more credence and respect regarding the management and control of their creative practice, the role of 'art director-illustrator' will transpire within the world of advertising.

UPPER CLASS SUITE   Now on all flights to Hong Kong. *Book at virgin.com/atlantic*

2

UPPER CLASS SUITE   Now on all flights to JFK. *Visit virgin.com/suite*

3

UPPER CLASS SUITE   Now on all flights to JFK. *Book at virgin.com/atlantic*

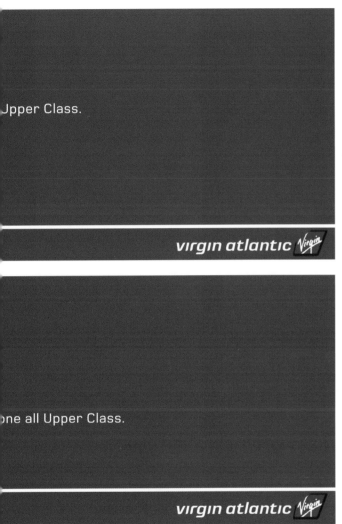

Jpper Class.

virgin atlantic *Virgin*

ne all Upper Class.

virgin atlantic *Virgin*

New York's gone all Upper Class.

virgin atlantic *Virgin*

5

4

1–4. Jonathan Williams provides award-winning imagery for this campaign to advertise the Upper Class Suite for a well-known airline. The imagery mixes clichés of British landed gentry with familiar aspects of trans-global destinations. These illustrations are gently subversive, yet challenge the perception of first class aviation whilst communicating a commitment to quality.

5. Lynda K. Robinson promotes attendance at a certain cabaret recital through this poster illustration.

1

172 Identity

'Below the Line' and Corporate Branding

The general essence of this context relates to aspects of brand and corporate recognition. What does that mean in relation to illustration practice and where and how does it manifest? Generally and contextually it can be considered an umbrella for a number of fairly disparate kinds of media placements with packaging and corporate identity being the chief aspects. In a business and professional practice sense it can be associated with notions of graphic design collaboration for the illustrator with a significant number of commercial projects of this nature being originated by design groups and studios.

The work undertaken is often referred to as being **below the line**. This description has its origins in advertising. It also implies that there is an **above the line**. Above the line is advertising in most of its manifestations, particularly where it is direct and focused. Below the line can be a direct association with the products or services being advertised, but does not actively promote. Instead, it provides a necessary and important supplement that ensures there is brand recognition and enhancement with packaging, point-of-sale literature and associated interactive material being important aspects of this process.

As well as product or service brand recognition, there must also be an important consideration for approbations related to its ownership: the company, organisation or manufacturer of its origin. This is frequently referred to as Corporate Identity. In many instances there are ubiquitous and recognisable symbols and images that immediately provide for the identity of a particular company or organisation. These 'badges' of organisation are normally referenced as **logos** with a visual form that is representative of the principal characteristic or ambience of the company and what it does. A logo can be evidenced in many visual forms from being fairly complex or decorative to a simple geometric juxtaposition of basic shapes reminiscent of the first letter of a company name. Indeed,

2

3

1,2. A set of postage stamps from 1960s Hungary giving a particular cultured labelling for the country by way of these equine pastimes. Postage stamps are often designed and illustrated in a contemporary context to extol an individual nation's identity and branding.

3. Anna-Louise Felstead provides a visually scenic overview of the work in progress associated with business pertained in the appropriately titled 'Tradefloor' brochure.

4. Clementine Hope's imagery for the cover of a company report is appropriately corporate in style and suggestion.

5,6. Branding for 'Kiss Radio' provided by Richard Duckett.

4

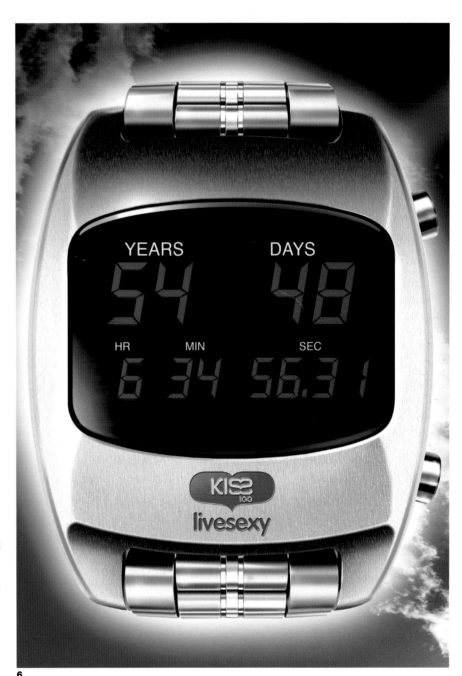

5

there are some instances where the logo assumes a stylised form of lettering; the British Virgin group of companies branding being an extremely recognisable example.

The logo is used in many ways, from print and online letter heading and correspondence, to large-format retail identity and recognition for company premises. The craft and intellectual capabilities of the illustrator are well placed to undertake logo design. Once the sole remit of the graphic designer, illustrators can equally process, assimilate and analytically conclude the appropriate direction to proceed relating to what the logo should provide regarding the specific corporate identity of an individual organisation. By possessing an inherent visual intelligence combined with conceptual and practical skills, a successful outcome should be determined by the illustrator.

Many companies seek the acquisition of additional corporate imagery in order to provide added flavour and a further projection of quality and enhancement to their status and standing. Some commission the design and production of 'paintings' – large conceptual illustrations providing a more in-depth corporate overview and often appropriated in reception areas and boardrooms. Sometimes elaborate and thought provoking and sometimes purely decorative, illustrations are frequently commissioned to enhance and provide a heightened sophistication to company annual and financial reports. Normally containing 'dry', complex statistics and charts, and accompanied by 'uncolourful' literature, these publications are transcended into fresh heights of visual 'good taste' by the inclusion of illustration and use of contemporary design sensibilities. The identity and 'branding' of sovereign states can be represented by the myriad of postage stamps extolling the culture and achievements of individual countries. An examination of the variety and richness of themes and designs will reveal an extensive and evocative use of illustration from years ago to the present day.

6

1

174

Point of Sale and an Overview of Packaging

Another feature firmly embedded as a component of below-the-line work is that of point of sale. Predominantly evidenced in situations of retail and promotion, this is material principally given for identification, visual enhancement, supplementary promotions and information related to products or services.

Some companies and organisations make considerable use of illustration in this context. Banks and building societies are no exception. Because of the formality and the intangible and abstract nature of finance, many will publish leaflets and other printed literature thematically designed and illustrated using examples that are the best regarding contemporary imagery and typography. The counters and other receptacles within these institutions are adorned with much to entice the customer to re-evaluate their mortgage lending, insurance contributions or investments. The illustrations contained within these leaflets are often graphically integrated with the text and have a large visual presence yet usually bear no relation to said products.

Other forms of point-of-sale material can be evidenced throughout the whole retail market. There are large cardboard edifices accompanying appliances for sale in hypermarkets, obtrusively indicating the location and proximity of your 'favourite'

2

3

1,4. Wine packaging, labelling and promotion can provide a rich source of work for the illustrator: a scan at supermarket or liquor store wine stocks will reveal evidence of much illustration being used. This illustration is by Russell Cobb.

2. Fashion branding and point-of-sale imagery for 'Oasis' clothes by Louise Hilton.

3,5. Richard Duckett's promotional images for these well-known confections clearly

display their own recognisable branding features and are used appropriately for both point-of-sale and advertising purposes.

6. This poster image by Nina Davis further enhances the reputation of the product by promoting 'essential' information to potential customers both inside and away from the retail outlet.

7. Martin Macrae gives an additional visual presence to this already recognisable brand identity.

4

5

make of flat-screen television. There are noisy and unduly noticeable interactive devices designed as play consoles to entice younger children into persuading their parents or guardian that a certain brand of digital device is a 'state of the art' must have.

These examples represent a cross section of elements that penetrate throughout the whole remit of point of sale.

Packaging is a branch of design practice given to the creative and appropriate use of illustration. Indeed, the craft of illustration is an ideal conveyance of the inclination that will place distance between a product and its competitors. The use of illustration can provide an idealisation of a product without conveying unnecessary falsehoods and without the sometimes alienating coldness and hyperrealism given by photography. An illustrator's inherent sense of visual language can enhance a seemingly mundane product, confer a contemporary guise and make it appealing to an appropriate and potential customer base. An example is children's foodstuffs where 'user friendly' humorous

6

7

'An illustrator's inherent sense of visual language can enhance a seemingly mundane product.'

1

176 and entertaining characterisations are utilised. The whole remit that is packaging has considerable diversity and can materialise in many forms and undertakings from vehicle livery, carrier bags and merchandise, toiletries, household goods and appliances.

Food and drink products in particular, make extensive use of illustration. Evocative and sensitive drawings can provide a natural and 'unforced' character, emphasising flavour and quality. Wine labels especially use illustration, often to project the characteristics of the place of origin.

2

1–4. Book publishers often utilise marketing and promotional material for in-store, catalogue and other placements. Richard Oliver has produced a series of images that promotes the re-release of Orwell's '1984': imagery that appropriately has an editorial and sophisticated texture.

6.12.98	Compte Gas\nde Chasseloup-Laubat	Jea...d	Achères	39.24
17.01.99	Camille Jenatzy	La Jamais Contente	Achères	41.42
17.01.99	de Chasseloup-Laubat		Achères	43.69
27.01.99	Camille Jenatzy	...ontente	Achères	49.92
04.03.99	de Chasseloup-Laubat	...d	Achères	57.60
29.04.99	Camille Jenatzy	...Jamais Contente	Achères	65.79
13.04.02	Leon Serpollet	Serpollet	Nice	75.06
05.08.02	William Vanc...	Mors	Ablis	76.08
05.11.02	Henri Fourn...		Dourdan	76.60
17.11.02	Augières		Dourdan	77.13
17.03.03	Arthur Du...		Ostend	83.47
05.11.03	Arthur		Dourdan	84.73
12.01.04	He...		...ake St Cla	91.37*
27.01.04			...ona B	92.30*
31.03.04				94.78
25.05.04				97.25
21.07.04				103.55
13.11.04				104.52
25.01.05				104.65*
30.12.05				109.65
23.01.06				121.57
08.11.09				125.95
16.03.10				131.27*
23.04.11	...			141.37*
24.06.14	L. G. ...			124.10
17.02.19	Ralph d...			149.87*
27.04.20	Tommy Milton			156.03*
17.05.22	Keneth Lee Guin...			133.75
	...omas			143.31
	...dge		Arpajon	146.01
	...bell		Pendine Sands	146.16
	...ll		Pendine Sands	150.76
			Southport	152.33

4

1

178   Books and Music

The jackets and covers of books are often an important and challenging aspect to the work of the illustrator. Although not immediately assumed as packaging, contextually the work of the cover is no different to that provided by the physical 'box' and associated visual identity given to any other product.

The overriding objective is for the illustrator to conceive and design an image that is consistent with and evocative of, the book's theme. Integration with the all important text that gives title and author is paramount and should be a prerequisite aspect of the design process.

The cover gives identity, like other circumstances of packaging, and functions as point of sale and marketing. It is therefore usual to consider a design solution that promotes a generic flavour. Specificality regarding any part of the book's content could be misleading. For example, a non-fiction publication extolling the rich variety of fauna and flora in any given earthly biome would send the wrong message if a single, obscure specimen appeared on the cover. Familiarity and understanding of the book's contents – the narrative or the essence of what is being said – is essential in order to ensure that an appropriate visual identity is utilised.

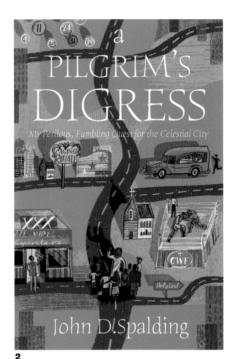

2

3

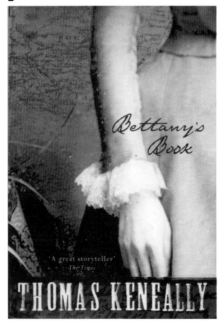

4

5

1,8. Jonny Hannah packages a book about Louis Armstrong with an illustration that also does well to promote the subject in question, provide narrative insights and give celebratory, editorial comment.

Four book covers depicting a variety of visual languages. The essence and success of these is borne out of illustrating a generic theme, yet providing a focused visual identity for the contents. Design and typographic appropriation are also essential elements for successful bookcover presentation.
2. Nigel Owen.
3. Jonny Hannah.
4. John Clark.
5. Andy Potts.

6. Sally Taylor has painstakingly rendered this image by traditional means, recreating the mosaic iconography associated with the book's theme. The titling is also part of the illustration.

7. Alex Williamson's original cover artwork image (minus titling) for a book entitled 'Rumblefish'.

5

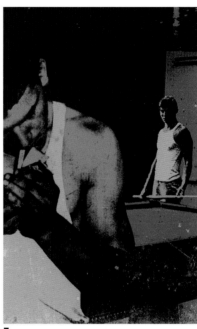

'The cover gives identity, like other circumstances of packaging, and functions as point of sale and marketing.'

6

7

8

1

180 The music industry has for many years been synonymous with creative and 'cutting edge' use of visual imagery. The sleeves of original vinyl, long playing records were considered an essential and iconic representation of contemporary taste and fashion. The pop, rock, progressive and psychedelic protagonists of the 1960s facilitated the design and illustration of record sleeves evocative of the bohemian and decadent ideals that challenged the established society. Indeed, the record packaging mirrored the essence of the performances and behaviour of the bands themselves. Although photographic, Jimi Hendrix's 'Electric Ladyland' is a classic example. Others provided opportunities for illustrators to become celebrated within the genre: Roger Dean became well known for producing fantasy-like and surreal landscapes, adorning the complete spreads of LP sleeves. Today, illustration continues to provide music with visual identity and form. The packaging of music and other forms of entertainment is now given to the compact disc and DVD. To a large extent, the long playing record, the cassette tape and video have been replaced. Currently, certain styles of illustration are appropriated because of their contemporary standing and empathic association with the music. However, such is the diversity of musical forms, from the many facets of jazz to the eclecticism of world music, the depth and spread of the visual language of illustration will facilitate visual identity for every genre in a fresh and innovative manner. Illustration is also ideally placed to package a contemporary recording of classical music. The works of the great classical composers are repeatedly recorded and one way to distinguish a new version is to give it a fresh, visual identity.

2

Three distinct music forms appropriately packaged by way of these illustrated CD covers and each duly representative of the genre in question:

1,2. Bonnie Dain re-casts a celebrated classical opus by providing this fresh identity; **3.** Monica Laita presents contemporary figurative interaction for 'Smooth Grooves'; **4.** Dave Kinsey's distinctly urban feel for the 'Dub Pistols'.

5–7. Rian Hughes has created a visual house-style for this series of audio-books, all written by the same author: An example of illustrator assuming responsibility for the overall design concept, including titling and visual content.

3

4

5

6

7

1

182   **Illustration and Design**

Within the remit of the contextual domain of identity and all of its manifestations, the illustrator is consistently engaged with the design process. It is unlikely that one would initiate and provide 'authorship' to any aspects of this context. However, the integrity of the illustrator is rarely diminished or challenged and one's conceptual and visual intelligence can be appropriated to its full extent.

It is usual for the brief to assume an element of prescriptivity with defined audiences and graphic constraints, such as an adherence to established house-styles.

Traditionally, the brief represents that initial stage where the aims and desires of the client are communicated to the illustrator. The brief is also the moment which establishes the nature of the client/illustrator relationship. In this instance, the client may be assumed as being the manufacturer or originator of the product or services in question. It may also be their appointed representative. In a professional practice context, the role of the illustrator should be as an innovative and vigorous partner and not a submissive or passive provider to the client. Dual direction debate rather than single-track orders brings about the most original solutions and freshest initiatives. Effective visual communication is not the result of some clandestine undertaking aiming to confuse, but instead a free and purposefully administrated process of imagination, analysis and professional bearance.

2

2. Dave Kinsey integrates design and illustration practice with these 1999 Burton Snowboards.

Three poster designs providing immediacy and clarity of information appropriating the visual language of stylised realism:

1,5. Laurence Whiteley's invitation to a wine tasting.

3. Bill Butcher's tobogganing extravaganza.

4. Steven Rydberg exemplifies best practice in illustration and design with this poster for Loring Café. An example of illustrator as graphic designer, this is an undertaking of both design and practical processes from client briefing to final media rendition. A tasteful and evocative composition, a concept that includes titling with imagery.

3

4

5

4

Appendix

186

Glossary

Airbrushed
An image that is comprised of super-fine and hyper-gradated tones and colours giving the illusion of precise yet exaggerated realism, particularly to mechanical subjects with shiny surfaces.

Allegorical Images
Narrative illustration that describes a subject that is under the guise of another. Imagery in which meaning is symbolically represented.

Ambient Imagery
Imagery that superficially surrounds or gives flavour without obvious or direct meaning.

Animatronics
Three-dimensional models that usually represent living entities and digitally or physically appropriated realistic movement and action.

Anthology
A defined selection of artworks or literature that is either thematic or originated by the same artist or author.

Art Director
A creative or media employee (publishing or advertising, etc.), who is senior in position and has responsibility for the design, production and quality of creative visual work. Normally assumes responsibility for the commissioning of illustration.

Artistic Licence
The creative freedom to re-interpret or re-designate aspects of visual work that is being undertaken.

Autographic
Imagery that is rendered by traditional means using drawing, painting and other studio-based techniques.

Avante-garde
Pioneering and innovative illustration or art, particularly that which is contemporary in its context. Term often used to describe that which 'pushes the boundaries'.

Cladogram
A type of diagram depicting evolutionary or generic relationships.

Collage
A technique or visual stylisation whereby an image is constructed either physically or digitally by mixing and gluing together various disparate elements such as photographs, drawings, abstract textures, etc.

Copywriter
An advertising or media creative who generates ideas for campaigns and prepares and writes words for publication or broadcast.

Creative and Media Industries
The world of publishing, television, advertising, multimedia, design, etc.

Decorative Imagery
That which uses elements of pattern, visual ornamentation or adornment and usually without any form of representation.

Digital Revolution
The emergence and impact of the computer regarding the generation of visual imagery and the subsequent changes and attitudes it has imposed on to working practice.

Diorama
A large, scenic image which is often used as a museum backdrop and having accompanying three-dimensional elements. Also used for film set purposes.

Fantastical Imagery
Extravagant and often wildly fanciful images, usually applied to narrative fiction. Fantasy illustration and science fiction are examples.

Fine Art
Paintings, sculptures, films or other visual entities, cultivated subjectively and often produced to express opinions or experiences of the artist. Normally accessed in its intended and original form, traditionally in galleries, but could be in any other prescribed venue or situation.

Frescos
Original images painted directly on to the surface of a wall or ceiling. Traditionally rendered in water colour before the plaster is dry.

Genre
In art generally, a specific style, kind or class. Within the discipline of illustration it describes a particular visual language.

Geometry
The drawing and visual representation of the properties and relations of magnitudes, such as lines, surfaces and solids in space.

Graph
A type of diagram that depicts the relation between two variable quantities.

Graphic Design
A generic term for an applied, creative, visual practice that incorporates the management and generation of concepts, ideas and finished design solutions for a number of media concerns and outlets such as print, publishing and multimedia. Contextually broad with practitioners often specialising in packaging, corporate identity, advertising and promotion, typography and web page design.

House-style
A thematic and graphic representation for a series of books (e.g. by the same author) or packaging for an associated range of products.

Iconic
Of an image; its nature or essence.

Iconography
The essence of pictures or images; personal style or visual language.

Juxtaposition
The placement of individual visual elements, either side by side or designed specifically to 'free float' within a graphic layout and not held by 'real space' or illusion of three-dimensionality.

Metaphorical Imagery
That which is imaginative, but not literally applicable; visual depiction of ideas or theories with accent on the conceptual as opposed to pictorial realism.

Moving Images
Generic term for animation (traditional and digital) and live-action filming.

Opacity
The application of an opaque medium rendered in a solid consistency, such as oil paint or gouache. The opposite of transparency.

Pastiche
An image produced in the style of another, usually of a well-known illustrator or artist.

Pictorial Representation
An image that represents 'real space'; an accurate depiction of a scene, usually literal in nature and not conceptual.

'Spot' Illustrations
Small free-standing images, vignette in nature and used mainly in an editorial context. Often surrounded by a typographic layout.

Stock Art 187
The assignation of secondary rights to images with potential mass use and exposure.

Surface Pattern
Imagery that is often repetitive and decorative in nature and used in textiles, fashion and interiors. Does not communicate contextually and should not be associated with illustration.

Symbolism
The use of signs and other visual, graphic characters to represent subjects; to visually express by suggestion.

Synopsis
A summary, proposal or outline.

Taxonomy
A system of classification that depicts inherent hierarchies.

Theorist-Practitioner
An individual who combines theory, research, and/or subject expertise with creative, design or craft-based practice.

Transferable Skill
A skill, either intellectual or practical, acquired through a specific course of study that can be utilised by employment within a different discipline, professional practice or sphere of operation.

Typographic
The use of type; printed/reproduced letterforms within graphic layout or concept.

Vista
A view of a scene; landscape imagery.

Visual Communication
The transfer of contextualised messages to prescribed audiences.

Visual Language
A style of illustration, either generic or associated with an individual illustrator.

Visual Syntax
The ability to construct and depict the appropriate connections and relationships with elements within illustration and design; visual literacy.

Volumatic Representation
A two-dimensionally rendered image that depicts three dimensions.

Education **Project Brief Development Checklist**

Establish:

The Rationale – What it is and reason for doing it
Do you have a suggested theme/topic or body of knowledge and have you identified a need for visual communication?
Has the inspiration and initiation of this project come from you or do you need to seek advice and be offered suggestions?
If you are floundering for ideas, are there personal interests or experiences that might provide inspiration or previous project work that could initiate a 'follow on'?
Are you playing to your strengths both intellectually and practically? Is there potential for you to excel?
Is there a defined context for the project, what is its thrust? Is the intention to inform, comment, promote, narrate etc.?
Do you understand, empathise, agree with or philosophise about the subject matter or theme?
Do you have sufficient depth of understanding to determine a suitable level of enquiry and analysis? Is the intended work intellectually challenging or is it lightweight?
Has a defined audience been established?
Is there an envisaged client or type of client?

Identify:

The Aim – What it is you intend to do
Have you determined a final outcome and what its form will be e.g. a children's book, an advertising campaign, a series of editorial commentaries, a research project, etc.?
Does the project or final outcome have a title?

The Objectives – How you intend carrying out the work
What intellectual skills do you need? How much research and analysis is required?
How much reference gathering is envisaged?
How much design work, conception of ideas or originality is needed in order for the project to succeed?
What practical skills are required? How much visual material is to be completed e.g. visuals, storyboards, artefacts, artworks etc.?
Have you established your own mini-curriculum or timetable in order to carry out the project? Is it realistic?

The Conclusion – The end result
Is there a defined deadline and date for completion? Are you being 'over-generous' with time allocated for this project?
What do you intend to gain or learn by undertaking this project?

Education   **Research and Reference Gathering Checklist**   **189**

The Internet
Public libraries
College/University libraries
Bookshops (new)
Bookshops (second-hand)
Photographic agencies
Museums
Other public organisations (e.g. local government departments, etc.)
Video/DVD/Film
Own reference photography
Sketchbook work
Miscellaneous primary sources (e.g. specialists, other places/individuals, etc.)

Education **Project Assessment and Review Checklist**

Theoretical

Analysis: depth of understanding regarding problem set.
Formulation of brief: appropriateness and rationale, range and level of intellectual challenges.
Problem solving: methodologies employed – research strategies, archival analysis.
Contextual understanding: Does the work communicate effectively to a prescribed audience?
Does it conform to the contextual task? Has it been properly researched and is the subject
matter/content accurate or appropriate regarding the project's aim?
Critique and reflection: depth of critical awareness and clarity of argument or thought.

Conceptual

Creativity and innovation: strength of, breadth and range of ideas, use of lateral and
imaginative processing.
Visual intelligence: application of design skills, visual literacy, appropriate use of aesthetics or
non-aesthetics, semiotics, visual metaphor, representation or symbolism.
Concepts: function and overall visual presence, interactivity and level of accessibility
regarding context or message being conveyed – does it 'work', is its media placement
appropriate (e.g. publishing, etc.), choice and utilisation of visual language.

Practical

Use of media, method, technique and process: quality of autographic and/or digital
rendering, technical concerns such as print reproduction.
Drawing and visualisation skills.

Professional

Organisation and time management: appropriate amount of work, adherence to time
schedule, use of initiative regarding general methodologies and problem solving, collation of
data and reference.
Presentation: artworks, presentation visuals, portfolio, exhibitions, etc.
Literacy: content and quality of all written work such as reports and briefs plus creative
material, such as copywriting or narratives.
Oral skills: standards of behaviour regarding academic debate, verbal presentation of work,
professional circumstances and general levels of communication.

Education**Project Appraisal, Critique and Reflection**191

Aspects to consider when compiling the project report

Title and Aims of Project.
Present the original rationale and state your inspiration or justification for doing the project.
Describe your methodologies in chronological order: research, collation of data and archival analysis, conceptual processes, media, practical and technical aspects, outcomes.
Identify any problems encountered and how they were solved.
Analyse and determine what you have learnt by undertaking this project. If aspects of the final outcome were not successful it is still possible to gain knowledge and experience that can facilitate future growth and attainment. You are assessed on what it is you have learnt, therefore it is essential to state as such.
Present a conclusion. Analyse, critique and reflect on the success of the completed work.
Reflect on your own performance from time management, problem solving to the creation of the final concepts.

It is essential to present a positive case as negative perceptions will send out the wrong signals:

 'I coloured it red – a terrible mistake – completely ruined – I hate it!'

 'In retrospect I think that green would have been a more appropriate colour because...'

192   **Project Proposal Proforma**

Project/Negotiated Programme Proposal
Name
Project Title
Date of Commencement
Rationale
Aim/s
Objectives
Proposed completion date
Signature
Tutor/Supervisor Signature

Professional Practice Issues   **The Illustrator's Representative (Agent)**   **193**

A great many illustrators considering a freelance career may think about representation. In fact, there are many successful and well-known illustrators whose careers have benefited enormously from this type of professional association. There is also a large number of named representatives who have successful companies that have been operating for years.

The majority function with integrity and professionalism and it can be widely regarded as saying that the advantages of representation outweigh the disadvantages.

In the United States they are commonly abbreviated to rep whilst in the United Kingdom they are referred to as agents. It is interesting to note that the majority of illustrator's reps occur in these two countries with Canada, the Netherlands and one or two other European countries having a few.

So what does a rep do? Their primary function is to promote you and get you work. They can be described as being a broker between illustrator and client, establishing the business parameters of a commission: the fee, costs and expenses, the deadline agreement and other practical arrangements, such as couriers for artwork delivery.

Here are some general guidelines:

Choose a rep that suits your own particular circumstance.

Some tend to specialise, for example only dealing with one type of client, such as advertising or publishing, or in subject matter.

Also, opt for a rep that you have a natural rapport with, as trust and reliability are extremely important. You may experience several reps before settling with one that suits you best.

Usually there is no legal binding or set contract. Make sure you know where you stand in terms of arrangements for payment; the relationship is based on the financial success of the partnership, which is the reason for it in the first place.

Reps all fulfil the same basic function, but there is not one that is the same.

They can vary considerably in size of operation and the nature of the work they represent. For example, there are some that may represent 60 to 80 illustrators with a staff number to match including secretarial and general help. Another may be a single-person operation with no more than eight to ten illustrators. Some represent a broad range of disciplines, such as general illustrators, animators, digital and multimedia people and photographers. Another may be special interest illustration only, such as cartoons or children's books.

A basic principle to remember is that it is in their interest to get you work. If you are not getting work then there is no benefit to either party, including them. They are a business and have to remain profitable to stay afloat.

194

Advantages

They take your portfolio around and find new clients.

They also show your work to people who might be seeing ten illustrators to commission one. This can save you a lot of time if you are one of the nine not chosen for the job.

They help in relation to fees because they know how to bargain.

They earn their commission and leave you more than you might have asked for. It is in their interest to negotiate the best possible deal for you.

They deal with the business side leaving the illustrator to concentrate on work.

This is an ideal situation for those who are uncomfortable having to chase up clients for money. The collection of payment can be an art in itself and can embarrass some illustrators. It never embarrasses reps.

They arrange publicity/promotion.

A sensitive rep will be able to give helpful advice about the development of your work, on commissions and help present your portfolio. Also, many reps have pages in promotional annuals such as 'The Directory of Illustration' and 'The Black Book'. It can be advantageous to have your work included in this way as these publications are distributed to a vast range of art directors from all types of organisations, such as publishing, advertising and multimedia. Having work on your rep's publicity pages may also help keep the price of the entry down as reps often share costs.

Good reps have a wealth of contacts and experience.

They can provide a good and broad snapshot of the current state of the industry because they will often know what sells and what does not. They will also know what illustration styles are 'in' and which ones are not.

For student graduates or others just starting out, to be offered representation can be an endorsement that your work is of a professional standard and appropriate for the current market in terms of style, content and direction. Also, being part of a group gives strength and credence to your position, particularly if there are some 'big names' associated.

A rep is a 'front man/woman' who can promote your talent to prospective clients in a way you may be reluctant to.

Good reps have considerable business acumen including the ability to do 'hard sell'.

They often make long distance trips abroad.

Many will endeavour to establish contacts with clients in potentially lucrative markets far and wide – for example, the whole of North America, Europe including the UK, Japan and the Far East.

They enable you as an illustrator to live more or less where you like.

Reps have access to numerous customers and many operate in cities such as New York or London where a majority of clients are. This enables you to live perhaps a considerable distance from a main client base and thus able to concentrate solely on your work.

Having a rep can simplify your bookkeeping, by providing regular statements of account prior to compiling your tax returns.

Disadvantages

They take a percentage commission.

Typical examples are 25%, 30%, 33% and 40%. The average is 30% for home-based work with an increase for overseas commissions.

You have to wait for the rep to pay you.

Some reps have a policy of making regular monthly payments for commissions irrespective of whether they have been paid or not – but not often. Usually you have to wait for the client to pay the rep and then the rep to pay you– minus their percentage commission. This can be a lengthy process.

They usually expect to have sole representation of your work.

Some reps are possessive of their illustrators and expect a commission on work you find yourself – fortunately not too many are in this category.

A basic convention of representation is that if you have established direct contacts with certain clients ensure that your rep knows who they are so as to avoid embarrassment – you do not want your rep going to a client promoting your portfolio when this particular art director has already given you the commission.

It is possible to have more than one rep especially if they are in different countries with unrelated client bases.

Having a different illustration style for each rep is also a possibility. Some illustrators have even been known to adopt a pseudonym for one of the styles they use.

A major problem with multirepresentation is that there may be difficulty in balancing how much work you do or take on. Your rep usually monitors your time management, particularly if you are in demand and have much interest in your work from potential customers.

You can become typecast.

If your portfolio has rat illustrations your rep could present you as the 'rat' person and nothing else may come your way – your rep should be prepared to present your wider abilities to prospective clients.

Also, some reps prefer to represent you as having one style as they would argue that it is easier for them to market you. Many art directors would not agree. If you are good at hyperreal natural history illustration, for example, and have equal ability at producing cartoons then it can make sense to employ you to do both, as you may be already familiar with the client and have a proven track record for reliability and professionalism.

Illustrators will often receive a brief direct from the rep without having an opportunity to talk to the client. This can lead to confusion and misrepresentation. You are the one doing the work so you should be the one discussing the job.

Some reps like to distance their illustrators from clients so you should always be clear as to the exact nature of what it is you are being commissioned to do.

It can sometimes lead to suspicion if your rep is not forthcoming about a client's identity. Fortunately this does not happen often, but they may be hiding information regarding fees or other important details.

196 **Professional Practice Issues**

The Illustrator's Portfolio

There are many ways in which illustrators promote themselves these days from producing printed material like books, flyers, visiting cards and posters; by subscribing to promotional annuals such as 'The Black Book' or 'The Directory of Illustration'; by producing an interactive CD or by showing work on a website.

The Web is an increasingly popular way for illustrators to introduce their work to potential clients. While a well-conceived and designed 'internet' site can be a very good vehicle to promote work, many art directors will agree that this is no substitute for the 'real thing' and will inevitably call in an actual portfolio.

So, in spite of modern technology it is the traditional portfolio that still does well to represent what you are about professionally and what you have to offer potential customers. It is your most important professional possession and no expense should be spared in putting it together and keeping it maintained and up to date.

Here are some general guidelines:

The overall look and content
Must be immaculately presented.

Avoid scruffy cardboard or office file type folders and buy proper professional leather or at least mock leather bound portfolios with clear acetate-like sleeves. A slick briefcase look is preferable to something overtly 'arty' and informal – no matter how bohemian you might be. No formalised shape or design is expected because the work should speak for itself. A portrait shape is generally acceptable, but it can be square or landscape providing all other criteria for preparing a professional portfolio are adhered to.

Don't go for a folder that is so elaborate it detracts from the work and select a colour that commands respect and authority – a dignified red, brown, blue or black is acceptable, but brilliant pink, orange and lime green are not.

It should not be too big.

It can look unprofessional and be physically awkward. Most art director's offices are small and inhibited spaces.

Must be physically durable.

Illustrators and reps frequently use public transportation and pavements as they travel through cities like New York and London – portfolios may be jostled around as they go from one appointment to the next. Your portfolio needs to be able to withstand this type of treatment without damage.

The first piece of work is very important
It sets a precedent for what follows. You are playing something of a psychological game, so don't start with a mediocre piece even if subsequent pages get progressively better. Whoever is reviewing your work will always expect to see more pieces like the first one. Start with an image that sets the tone and the overall standard.

The order of work should be appropriate for what you want your folder to do under different circumstances
You should adopt a flexible approach and establish contents where the order can be easily changed. If you are aiming for a specific commission or employment then that kind of work should be in the front. For example, if a potential client wants to buy natural history illustration then don't put that type of work at the back.

Design layout – think 'book-like'
Be consistent regarding overall presentation. There should be an easy pace and flow to the way the work is sequenced. Jumping from one style to another can be uncomfortable. It is acceptable to have more than one style (several even) – versatility may be your selling point – just make sure everything holds together harmoniously.
Keep all work squared up, positioned similarly and facing the same direction where possible. Persistent turning of the folder can also be irritating.

Don't overdo mounting
Don't use heavy mounting board. Keep to paper or thin card stock, otherwise your portfolio will look and feel unwieldy. Mount work on a neutral colour, preferably white as that simulates the pages of a book. Colour surrounding an image can affect and change its meaning or context. Work should be spray mounted to the page. Framing elements can be distracting.

Show work in context
If you are a published professional, show the printed/reproduced work – the pages from books or magazines, covers of books, stamps, corporate material, TV or animation stills. Students should also try to show work in context by preparing a mock-up of unpublished work. Remember, you are often demonstrating creativity, ideas and concepts as well as your technique and drawing ability.

Don't put original artwork in your portfolio
What would you do if your portfolio was lost or stolen? Traditionally produced paintings and drawings are too valuable, but easily duplicated digital images are acceptable to include. Some illustrators work big, using oil on canvas for instance. Oversized works should be professionally reproduced to fit the portfolio – it would most likely be printed much smaller for actual use.

Quality overrides quantity
Try not to use work that all look alike. Whoever is reviewing your portfolio might think that is all you can do. Most illustrators would not want to be pigeonholed. Also, the actual amount of work in a portfolio depends on the individual – there is no real convention or rule. However, too much can be tedious or even boring, and too little can give the impression that you don't have much experience or that most of what you do is not up to standard.

Duplicate portfolios
It is advisable to keep a duplicate portfolio as a 'hedge' against potential loss. There are occasions when it is only possible to 'drop off' your folder because some art directors don't have the time to see people face to face. It is also worth having this additional portfolio in case you need to see another potential client in the meantime.

198 **Professional Practice Issues**

Fees and Payments

This is an important issue for all freelance illustrators and one that causes more anxiety and concern than any other.

Arrangements about money should always be completely clear before you start any commission. But, before examining the details, what determines the worth of a job and why does the same size, complexity and standard finish for an artwork fetch a higher fee for one type of client over another? In fact, there are no rules about what a job is worth, but the bigger and more prestigious the client, the bigger the money. If the commission means that your work will have national and/or international exposure, as opposed to a local or regional outlet, then it is obvious which will pay most. You can demand the highest price for work in advertising with editorial commissions (magazine work) coming bottom of the scale.

There is a downside to working in advertising in spite of the high fees. The brief is often very prescribed, involving much direction and revision, and a short period of time to do the job. Editorial work can mean much more creative freedom.

In publishing there is generally a range of set fees, regardless as to which illustrator is used because a big book project, such as an encyclopaedia, may demand hundreds of images. Illustrating a complete children's book will normally command royalties and an advance. Please refer to the pricing guide on page 201.

The art directors who normally commission illustrators will sometimes have total control over the monetary side. For example, if they are responsible for the design of multi-imagery printed corporate material they will prepare a budget for the typographic content, artwork costs, reproduction, as well as for any illustrations used. This estimate is presented to the client, together with the design fee, before work commences.

An art director on a large magazine may not work as closely with the financial aspects. There is usually an annual rolling budget, which will have to be respected. Someone in authority will soon intervene if the budget is overstepped, but this will not affect the day-to-day commissioning because, as in book publishing, a set range of fees operates.

On small, localised publications the budget may be operated on a week-by-week basis – a low cost week could be followed by an expensive production the next week, while overspending on one issue would mean fewer illustrations in the next.

With regards to freelance, professional illustration practice, there are extreme categories of operation and this can have a bearing on payments and the understanding of the following:

199

Quality and reputation
a. A new illustrator who didn't make a name at college, who is starting from scratch, working away from major business centre.
b. An internationally known star name whose work has had public recognition regarding honours, prizes, awards, etc.

Calibre of clients
a. Someone who has yet to find enough clients and what clients he/she has prefer to spend as little as possible even dispensing with a professional illustrator altogether.
b. An illustrator who can afford to turn away clients of the wrong kind, with a body of clients who are prepared to take illustration seriously and who see themselves in the market for the very best.

How quickly you work
a. An illustrator who is still working out how to tackle commissions, who is constantly having to face problems not encountered before, who makes several false starts and who consequently may take a long time to complete a piece of work.
b. An illustrator who works fast as a result of years of experience in tackling every sort of problem.

Your financial toughness
a. Someone who hates dealing with the money side, would rather be 'ripped off' than haggle, basically committed to work rather than fees.
b. Someone who takes pride in financial acumen, hard bargaining, tight financial control and very high profits.

Overhead costs
a. Low-cost operation using whatever space available at home, buying only basic equipment, avoiding non-essential costs.
b. Someone with lavish premises in, for example, central New York or London with generous space, lavish equipment, high standard of living in studio.

200

The main points to establish regarding fees when commissioned to undertake a freelance illustration job are as follows:

How much for conceptual development and subsequent sketches/visuals?

How much is the total fee (including finished artwork)?

Are expenses included in total fee or an extra (necessary travel, reference acquisition, photography and/or printing, postage/packing/courier services, etc.)?

Are you paid for any changes to the artwork?

Is there a rejection fee or do you get the full fee if you complete the job to standard whether it is used or not?

Splitting the fees into concepts/sketches and final artwork depends on how much work you do at each stage. If you do most work at the concept stage you should try and organise (in advance) for a higher proportion of the fee to be paid for the work at this point if it is rejected. Make sure rejected sketches are your property.

Rejection is a difficult business. It is not simply a case of a bad piece of work going unpaid. If an illustrator has not achieved what was expected, then the client will have to accept at least part of the responsibility for not having briefed or supervised the work properly and must agree a mutually acceptable settlement. If an article in a magazine is dropped or an advertising campaign changed, for example, the art director has an obligation to honour the full fee.

Unlike graphic designers, illustrators are very rarely paid an hourly rate. You are quoted and paid a fee based on the overall completed job irrespective of the time taken or working practices involved.

And finally, the overall fee for the commission is for the use of the image as specified in the contract (e.g. book cover, magazine spot, etc.) – you retain the copyright and the original artwork.

Some basic guidelines for illustration pricing: **201**

Books

Trade paperback cover (large distribution): £700–2,000/$1,500–4,000
Trade hardback cover wraparound (large distribution): £1,600–3,000/$3,000–6,000
Interiors (large distribution) spread: £700–1,500/$1,500–3,500
Interiors (large distribution) spot: £160–400/$300–750
Children's book (24–32 page): £1,500–6,000/$3,500–12,000 advance + royalties 3%
paperback, 5% hardback

Advertising

Consumer magazine (large circulation) spread: £3,000–6,000/$6,000–12,000 (single image)
Newspaper (large circulation) quarter page: £700–1,500/$1,500–3,000 (single image)
Point of purchase (large printing): £1,500–4,500/$3,000–8,000
Direct mail cover: £1,500–4,500/$3,000–8,000

Editorial

Newspapers (large circulation) spot: £120–400/$250–700
Consumer magazine (large circulation) spot: £200–400/$350–700
Consumer magazine (small circulation) spot: £80–200/$150–400

Corporate

Annual report (large circulation) spread: £1,300–3,500/$2,500–6,500
Annual report (small circulation) spot: £80–450/$150–800

Source: 'The Graphic Artists Guild Handbook of Pricing and Ethical Guidelines' and author's
own professional experience.

202   **Notes & Sketches**

_____

_____

_____

_____

_____

_____

_____

_____

_____

_____

_____

_____

_____

_____

_____

_____

_____

_____

_____

_____

_____

_____

_____

_____

_____

_____

Notes & Sketches

204   **Notes & Sketches**

_____

_____

_____

_____

_____

_____

_____

_____

_____

_____

_____

_____

_____

_____

_____

_____

_____

_____

_____

_____

_____

_____

_____

Notes & Sketches

Notes & Sketches

_____

_____

_____

_____

_____

_____

_____

_____

_____

_____

_____

_____

_____

_____

_____

_____

_____

_____

_____

_____

_____

_____

_____

_____

Notes & Sketches

Notes & Sketches

_____

_____

_____

_____

_____

_____

_____

_____

_____

_____

_____

_____

_____

_____

_____

_____

_____

_____

_____

_____

_____

_____

_____

Notes & Sketches

_____

_____

_____

_____

_____

_____

_____

_____

_____

_____

_____

_____

_____

_____

_____

_____

_____

_____

_____

_____

_____

_____

_____

_____

General index

Illustrators index

Bibliography   Selected Reading

Steven Heller & Marshall Arisman
The Education of an Illustrator
Allworth Press/School of Visual Arts, 2000

Dale M. Willows
The Psychology of Illustration
Springer-Verlag New York, 1987

Evelyn Goldsmith
**Research into Illustration: An Approach
and a Review**
Cambridge University Press, 1984

Graham Vickers
**Illuminations: Solving Design Problems
Through Illustration**
Elfande Art Publishing, 1993

Tamsin Blanchard
Fashion and Graphics
Laurence King Publishing, 2004

Mario Pricken
Creative Advertising
Thames & Hudson, 2002

Leo Duff & Jo Davis (Ed)
Drawing: The Process
Intellect Books, 2005

Howard J. Smagula
Creative Drawing
Laurence King Publishing, 2002

J.G. Heck
The Complete Encyclopaedia of Illustration
Merehurst Press, 1988

Elaine R. S. Hodges (Ed)
The Guild Handbook of Scientific Illustration
Van Nostraad Reinhold, 1989

Stephen J. Gould, Chris Sloane & Alice Carter
The Art of National Geographic
National Geographic, 1999

Roanne Bell & Mark Sinclair
**Pictures and Words: New Comic Art and
Narrative Illustration**
Laurence King Publishing, 2005

Sylvia S. Marantz
The Art of Children's Picture Books
Garland Publishing, 1995

Kevin S. Hile
**Something About the Author: Facts and
Pictures About Authors and Illustrators of
Books for Young People**
Gale Group, 1994

Berthe Amoss & Eric Suben
**Writing and Illustrating Children's Books
for Publication: Two Perspectives**
Writer's Digest Books, 1995

Organisations

D&AD

Communication Arts

Society of Illustrators

Society of Children's Book Writers and Illustrators

Guild of Natural Science Illustrators

AOI

216

Acknowledgements

This book could not have become a reality without the considerable hard work and design skills of Peter Bennett. I also thank Clare Elsom for the diligence and professionalism given for the image research. Special thanks to Nina for the typing.

I owe a great debt to the many who have donated imagery and would like to thank the following for their generous and invaluable contribution to this book:

My colleagues at University College Falmouth who also teach on the BA(Hons) Illustration course:
Sue Clarke, Mark Foreman, Gary Long, Nigel Owen, Serena Rodgers, Linda Scott and Susan Boafo who teaches on the BA(Hons) Photography course.

Former and current students from the BA(Hons) Illustration course at University College Falmouth:
Joel Stewart, Jonathan Gross, Juan Moore, Jason Cripps, David Bain, Christopher Burge, Levi Pinfold, Greg Reed, Yee Ting Kuit, Eivind Bøvor, Juliet Percival, Hannah Cumming, Tom Haskett, Katherine Child, Arthur de Borman, Jessica Allen, John Aggs, Elizabeth Clements, Alys Jones, Fey Dodson, Thomas Plant, Richard Stanley, Ruth Thomlevold, Kirsty Thomson, Marjorie Dumortier, Hannah McVicar, Oliver Hurst, Emma Dibben, Rose Forshall, Sarah Horne, Tom Frost, Beth Knowles, Martin Wallace, Eleanor Rudge, Rebecca Riley, Jesse Mitchell, Katy Wright, Joseph Theobald, Chris Odgers, Eivind Gulliksen, Mandy Field, Kosei Kawakubo, Sally Taylor, and John Clark.

Joe Najman and the following artists represented by NB Illustration, London
www.nbillustration.com
Martin Macrae, Roger Harris, Richard Duckett, Jonathan Burton, Ben Hasler, Jo Goodberry, Graham White, David Young, Stephen Lee, Owen Sherwood, Clementine Hope, Asa Andersson, Yannick Robert, Sarah Nayler, Laurence Whiteley, Stephane Gamain, Louise Hilton, Nina Davis, Alasdair Bright, Marco Schaaf, and Judy Stevens.

Antonio Adriao and the following artists represented by American Artists Rep. Inc., New York
www.aareps.com
Jacques Fabre, Jerry LoFaro, Jean-Claude Michel.

The following individual illustrators:
Maria Raymondsdotter, Paul Hess, Chris Griffen, Andy Smith, Andy Bridge, Frazer Hudson, Neil Packer, Ricci Kawai, Lewis Campbell, Jill Calder, Richard Borge, Brad Holland, David Ho, Etienne Delessert, Wilson McLean, Victoria Rose, David Lesh, Joel Nakamura, Alana Roth, Joanne Glover, Lorena Pugh, Gary Cooley, Andrew Hutchinson, Steven Rydberg, Peter Kuper, Gary Baseman, Marina Sagona, Dave Kinsey, Jaime Zollars, Marq Spusta, David Aronson, Phil Kenning, Alberto Guerra, Anita Kunz, John Fox, Paul Bowman, John S. Cuneo, Liz Lomax, Lucy Truman, Ann Boyajian, Martin Rowson, Vicki Behringer, Michelle Thompson, Nick Hardcastle, Jamie Smith, John Bradley, Erik Wayne Patterson, Tom Gauld, Graham Dury, James Vinciguerra, Mark Hess, Brian Grimwood, Rafal Olbinski, Jonathan Williams, Lynda K. Robinson, Anna-Louise Felstead, Russell Cobb, Richard Oliver, Jonny Hannah, Andy Potts, Alex Williamson, Rian Hughes, Monica Laita, Bonnie Dain, Bill Butcher, and Gemma Robinson.

Special Credit for the Following:
Alan Male, Cover Illustration 'Insect Body Parts' – Heinemann Educational; Alan Male, 'Oceans' – Readers Digest Assoc; George Cruikshank (British, 1792–1878), The Burglary, 1838, 10.2 x 9.8 cm (image), 23.9 x 13.8 cm (sheet), Fine Arts Museum of San Francisco, Achenbach Foundation for Graphic Arts, 1963.30.32698; Saul Bass, 'One, Two, Three', ©1961 Metro-Goldwyn-Mayer Studios Inc. All Rights Reserved. Courtesy of MGM CLIP+STILL; Lewis Campbell – RCA Animation; Juliet Percival – Firefly Film and Television Productions Channel Four; Joseph Theobold – Bloomsbury Publishers; Paul Hess 'Hungry! Hungry! Hungry' – Malachy Doyle and Anderson Press; Susan Boafo – Research into Art Nature & Environment. Funded by Arts Council of England, University College Falmouth and the Environment Agency; Fey Dodson – fey_dodson_8@hotmail.com; Marina Sagona – Riley Illustration; Bonnie Dain and Ann Boyajian – Lilla Rogers Studio; Bill Butcher – www.billbutcher.com; Randolph Caldecott – www.randophcaldecott.org.uk; Graham Dury – Viz magazine, Fulchester Industries/Dennis Publishing; Monica Laita and Lucy Truman – New Division; Dave Kinsey – ©2006 Dave Kinsey, www.kinseyvisual.com; Andrew Hutchinson – Illustration Ltd.; Jamie Smith 'Everybody's Helper' – Readers Digest Assoc. Inc. 2006; Phil Kenning – www.kenning-illustration.co.uk; Vicki Behringer – www.courtroomartist.com; Lynda K. 'Barley' Robinson – CabaretSongRecords@amserve.com; Brian Grimwood – www.briangrimwood.com; Mark Foreman 'Grandpa Jack's Tattoo Tales' – Farrah, Straus & Giroux Publishers; Martin Rowson – mrowson2@hotmail.com.

Finally, thanks to Natalia Price-Cabrera and AVA Publishing SA without whom, this publication would not have been possible.